MARKETING STRATEGIES FOR THE ONLINE INDUSTRY

Marketing Strategies for the Online Industry

FREDRIC SAUNIER

G.K. Hall & Co. · Boston, Massachusetts

MARKETING STRATEGIES FOR THE ONLINE INDUSTRY

Fredric Saunier

Copyright 1988
by G.K. Hall & Co.
70 Lincoln Street
Boston, Massachusetts 02111

Printed on acid-free paper
and bound in The United States of America

10 9 8 7 6 5 4 3 2 1

Library of Congress Cataloging-in-Publication Data

Saunier, Fredric B.
  Marketing strategies for the online industry.

  (Professional librarian series)
  Bibliography: p.
  Includes index.
  1. Information storage and retrieval
systems—Marketing.   2. Information services—
Marketing.   3. Data bases—Marketing.   I. Title.
II. Series.
Z699.3.S28   1988   025'.040688   88–1227
ISBN 0–8161–1863–9
ISBN 0–8161–1879–5 (pbk.)

To
Anne Marshall Saunier

CONTENTS

List of Illustrations

INTRODUCTION

This book is intended to give a general picture of marketing practice in the electronic publishing industry. I have concentrated on defining and characterizing marketing. In an attempt to keep this book within reasonable limits, I have treated various aspects of my subjects with brevity, for example, the elements that make up pricing and the various styles of marketing in the industry. (The former is "a forest of intricate detail" and the latter is a study in its own right.) In all cases a fuller presentation would take more pages than can be afforded. From those who find parts of my presentation too brief, I beg indulgence.

My three main themes are:

1. THE ISSUE OF UNDERMARKETING

Historically, electronic publishers in the United States and Britain have underbudgeted, underspent, and, occasionally, misspent on marketing. These practices distort the relationship between marketing-induced productivity and the total revenue and market potential of the industry. Spotty marketing performance boosts the stock of the industries' technical performance to an exaggerated level of importance. It is said that technology drives the online industries' growth. Exactly how is never explained. The technology/motivation cycle helped build the online industry, just as it helped build the computer industry. Like the computer industry, the online industry will lose ground unless it too learns how to market and sell in an environment where technology is no longer glamorous and the buyer is just a common citizen.

The time is ripe for hard thinking and fresh appraisals. Over the last two years, as growth in the online industry has leveled out, marketing's star has begun to rise. In the United States, price inelasticity is a growing problem in many, if not most, online markets. In some organizations marketing is getting a new appraisal from online management because marketing programs can deal systematically and creatively with issues like price inelasticity. Also, as prices increase some services experience a corresponding decrease in the amount they are used. When revenue losses from all sources are combined with the cost savings to buyers from new online search efficiencies, product enhancements, the positive learning curves of important customers, and other developments favoring the buyer, the revenue patterns of some firms have altered. Many firms find that their established online markets can't be made to pay off as they once did. Total industry revenue still grows, and, most marketers agree, revenue can be expected to continue to grow in the future; growth will come increasingly from new marketing initiatives to gain market share rather than from new rounds of price increases or by the deployment of any foreseeable (or affordable) new online technologies.

2. THE ISSUE OF MARKETING EFFICIENCY

Across the industry the role and importance of marketing in the online organization is ready to grow or is already growing to new levels. The change is due to economics. A marginal revenue limit may exist in the online industry after all: it has often been argued that none existed given the runaway success of the specialized database services. If margins are found to be bounded, online organizations must learn to manage the costs of increasing output and doing business effectively while, at the same time, increasing their marketing efficiency and sales effort. Marketing increasingly appears as a major portion of the total expense of increasing the sales and revenues of any online organization. This is not because new, bigger, or better marketing is being done or even that marketing expenses are rising to new plateaus, but because a spread-sheet phenomenon has happened where the ratios for costs of hardware and other investments in the online "factory" itself are receding, leaving marketing expenses more exposed. Whether this new visibility will reveal to management the seemingly "hidden" value of marketing remains to be seen. Online managements are demanding more efficiency for their marketing money and they want it spent in specific primary, secondary, or tertiary markets. Marketing must respond and deliver in these markets.

3. THE ISSUE OF CREATIVE EXCELLENCE

The reader might well ask why creative excellence is a major issue in a volume on marketing. One reason is that most of the firms in the online industry do not have sales forces; they rely on their marketing communication programs for sales. Another reason is that too much marketing communication opportunity is being wasted because of poor creative decision making and execution. Therefore, the theory and practice of marketing communications in the industry is examined with the intention of stimulating the reader's interest in and mastery of communication theory and practice.

The examples in this book show that creative excellence in marketing communications is neither easy to obtain nor cheap, yet the result always pays back the conceptual effort and expense. The creative review covers material as diverse as direct mail and international advertising, over fifty examples in all. These examples show the overall level of work in the industry, and, collectively, they are a useful, and sometimes cautionary, idea file for the manager and marketer.

A CLIMATE OF CHANGE

The themes mentioned above are being acted out in an industry environment of changing expectations. Andrew Pollock, writing in the September 15, 1987, *New York Times*, says,

The vision of an electronic society in which consumers read the news, pay bills and make airplane reservations on their home computers has proved illusory.

People still seem to prefer touching the merchandise in a department store to ordering by computer, and reading a newspaper to scanning a video display tube with their morning coffee. Moreover, computerized information services have been costly and confusing to use, leading to numerous failures by companies that attempted to introduce them.

Last week, a Federal judge tried to start the nation moving again toward realizing this vision. Judge Harold H. Greene, who presided over the breakup of the Bell telephone system, ruled that local telephone companies created by the 1984 breakup could provide billing and transmission services that would make it easier for consumers to use such information systems, often known as videotex.

Few nascent industries have ever been saddled with such universally high growth expectations as has the online industry, but today the industry growth curve is relatively flat, expectations are falling, and disappointment is spreading. Few new services and products have ever attracted such a fascinating and diverse group of able and imaginative product developers and marketers as the online industry had at the outset. Yet the charge of mediocrity in marketing and corporate leadership and management is now bandied about so often that it no longer sounds like sour grapes. Many of the most urbane, intelligent, creative, and humane managers and marketers have left the industry, vowing never to return.

Marketing in some sectors of the online industry is in trouble: in some firms marketing has never been well liked, trusted, or even understood by online management; in others, marketing's "push" in the market is compared disparagingly and illogically to the market "pull" of the online technology itself; and, in many organizations, the marketing department is not at all sure of the quality and potency of its body of market knowledge, philosophy, tools, techniques, and creativity. There are a number of organizations in the industry where marketing focused on price-sensitive and price-inelastic markets in the early years: one of the consequences of that kind of limited marketing history is that many of the marketing lessons coming out of the marketing of other high tech services and products have gone unnoticed.

There are both old and new lessons to be considered, tested, and, in some cases, relearned. As marketers put their creative energies into new markets, operating under conditions of bounded revenue margins, they will find themselves working with scarce resources. I attempt to strengthen the practice, efficiency, and success of marketing in the online industry by enlarging on marketing and industry issues like those listed above, looking at what is being done, and speculating on what might be done. In making suggestions about the role of marketing, I call for an expanded marketing point of view and organization, but not at the expense of technology or product development. What I see most clearly is the value of a productive alliance of peers.

1

THE ELECTRONIC PUBLISHING INDUSTRY

1.1. The Online Information Systems of the Private Sector Grew Out of the Modernization of Publishing and in the Last Decade Have Become Electronically Propagated Alternatives and Additions to Traditional Information Search and Retrieval Techniques.

INFORMATION GROWTH

Since the end of World War II there has been a world-wide explosion of knowledge. The pressures for better organization and management of data and information for the purposes of research and analysis in government, knowledge institutions, and elsewhere grew dramatically as the total of all information in existence before the war doubled, and then doubled again within a decade or so. It was inevitable that automation would be applied in many different ways to this problem. The first touch created modern business legend. One version of the story is that when IBM offered its early machines to banks and other high volume data users, it found no takers. IBM was in financial trouble when a librarian attending a dinner party where she was told about the machines by Thomas Watson, the founder of IBM, asked if the library could see one. It did, and the first IBM customer was a library whose management saw the value of being able to store and manipulate data by automated means. IBM was saved and the age of data automation dawned.

So far as I can determine, there is no direct line of technical descent from early IBM installations to today's electronic databases and systems, but the first application of data automation in a knowledge institution is significant: it shows the growing magnitude of data management issues in knowledge institutions and the basic appeal of automation.

PAPER PUBLISHING

In the 1960's the digital computer started to turn up everywhere in business and government, automating different activities. Publishing was economically and technically ripe for automation. Publishing requires typesetting to get print on paper, and the wood and metal typefont systems used in both the composing room and the print shop had remained fundamentally unchanged for about 500 years. When the computer and other new technologies arrived in the composing room and print shop, paper publishers found them attractive. They switched to computerized photographic typesetting because the new systems generated preproduction materials better suited to modern platemaking and printing processes.

As part of the new typesetting process, computers made a complete magnetic record on computer tape of each typeset text. The production of large numbers of high quality, machine-readable tapes, each containing a full transcript of important texts, introduced a technology of potential commercial value—the tapes were suitable for computer-based storage and retrieval of information, a new process which had already been shown to be feasible by the government.

DATABASES COMPOSED OF TAPES

The development of the database technique of storage and retrieval fit into the demand for better data and information management to support the manual processes of the storage and retrieval of information. In database storage a collection of tapes on the subject of agronomy, for example, is organized in a large electronic file called the agronomy database, which is, by definition, a collection of information (about agronomy) organized in a form that can be accessed and processed by a computer system.

The first electronic databases in operation were in the government's military, intelligence, and research communities; this was a natural development because they had a built-in need for the distribution and analysis of large quantities of data and their own resident computers could be used. An initial justification for government databases was that there was a predetermined ready-made audience, an existing "market" in government and its allied knowledge institutions that would get a higher knowledge payoff from automated storage and retrieval. Also, there was a tradition of government-sponsored information centers whose staff and data holdings lent themselves readily to automation and electronic networking. Similar markets of users in the private sector had to be envisioned and developed by expensive and painstaking marketing activities: the payoff for the user had to be convincingly planned, paid for, and well demonstrated long in advance of product and service introduction.

THE ELECTRONIC PUBLISHERS

Corporations contracted with paper publishers for the rights to distribute the texts encoded on their tapes. Not all early databases were built by this technique however. Some of the most successful were constructed from original information sources solely for the purpose of being sold electronically. Others had a connection with the government at one point but ended up in the private sector. Regardless of the origins of the database, a private sector database owner maintains a computer-driven method for finding all of the specific information in the databases available on the computer (and sometimes on the computers of others by an access technology called a gateway). He also markets access to the databases to those who need data and information.

These businesses are called *vendors,* and vendor companies are the basic business units of the online industry. Since they sell information electronically, they are classified as *electronic publishers* or *parallel publishers.* It is not clear whether vendors sell a product (a piece of information taken from a database either by electronic means or on paper) or a service (access to and delivery of a quantity of information in the database), or both. Regardless of which way it is conceived, an electronic publisher adds value to the information and data sold.

THE VENDOR'S APPROACH

The vendors loaded the databases on mainframes, massive computing machines with the speed and storage capacity to handle high volumes of data, and, at the same time, work with many teletype-like terminals, each with direct access to the data. The vendors added powerful search software to their mainframes that permitted fast, accurate, systematic retrieval of the stored data. This system created a highly valuable commercial possibility: charging a fee for quickly finding specific information on demand—automated searching—in a mode that allowed the user the personal freedom to search a database from any place a properly equipped terminal happened to be located.

(mainframe) + (databases) + (search software) + (access terminals) = (vendor's automated information system)

Figure 1.1. The vendor's operational scheme.

PRODUCT DEVELOPMENT

By building large collections of tapes into databases, often from many different paper publishers, vendors were able to bundle databases into specialized knowledge products. Some of the first were for government agencies, while others were for lawyers, stock brokers, and librarians. Over the years dozens of private and public specialized knowledge products have been built in the United States, Great Britain, Japan, and elsewhere.

Specialized knowledge products are expensive. For them to be widely useful and to earn return on investment, access had to be expanded beyond the users of terminals wired to the mainframe. Since mainframes are expensive to own and run and terminals are cheap, a network of terminals made sense. When the idea caught on, cheap terminals would automatically deploy into a large diffuse system thereby solving the revenue problem.

SERVICE DEVELOPMENT

This business plan was implemented by using the existing electronic packet-switching networks already in use by other businesses and adapting their software, standards, and protocols to control online communications. By the early 1960's remote data processing networks had evolved to the point where this was a practical move. RDP networks had begun operations in the late 1950's to meet the needs of remote data processing users such as branch banks that needed to send their daily numbers to their home office computers.

The step was obvious: remote data processing networks permitted remote terminals to tap a database in the vendor's mainframe.

Today almost anyone, anywhere in the world, who is equipped with a modern telephone, a computer with a modem, a subscription to the vendor's database, the proper entry and access passwords, operator instruction, and terminal software can query a remote database via an international open-access, packet-switching network. Examples of such networks are TYMNET, Telenet, or Uninet in the United States, and British Telecom PSS in Britain.

(vendor's database systems) + (packet-switching network) + (properly equipped remote terminals) + (user instruction) = (wide access to the vendor's automated information databases)

Figure 1.2. The vendor's database access scheme.

USING A DATABASE

After a connection is established between a mainframe and the customer's terminal, questions can be put to the databases in the form of searches. Search software on the mainframe ensures that properly framed questions will get specific answers if the data are in the database and the question is properly framed. The line between terminal and mainframe is kept open during database searching, which normally takes only a few seconds. Search results are transmitted directly and exclusively to the terminal (screen or printer) of the user who asks the question and pays for the search.

SAMPLES OF ONLINE ACTIVITIES

The description of an online system in action, shown in figure 1.3, is taken from a CompuServe brochure, entitled "Now Get More Out of Any Computer with CompuServe." Founded in 1969, CompuServe is a United States "information utility," an information and data "department store" like Prestel in Britain (as opposed to a "boutique" online system with just one or two types of specialized data and information in its databases). CompuServe, with 380,000 subscribers in 1987, used widely by both business and the public, has found a way of making its system usable that works for hundreds of thousands of users. The activity shown below illustrates both the "menu-driven" and the "command-driven" methods for sending an electronic mail message (called EMAIL below) to another user of the online system. (One of the largest United States online companies does nothing but handle electronic mail.)

How to access a topic from the menu. Let's say you want to send someone a message via EMAIL. Just dial the CompuServe access telephone number for your area: connect the phone to your modem (the device that connects your computer to your phone) and enter your User ID number and password when your computer asks you to.

This is the first full (main) menu that will appear on your screen:

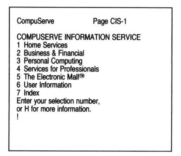

Now select #1, and this will appear on your screen:

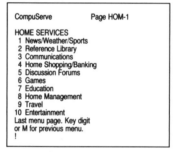

Now select #3, and this will appear on your screen:

Now select #1, and this will appear on your screen:

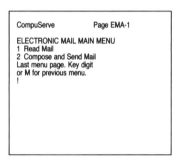

Since you do want to continue, press the "S" or *Enter* key, and this will appear on your screen:

And now you're ready to send your EMAIL message to any CompuServe subscriber.

How to take the shortcut. It is also possible to skip these steps and simply type in GO followed by the appropriate page code for whatever CompuServe topic you'd like to access.

In this case, to use EMAIL, you'd just type in GO EMA and press the *Enter* key when you see the ! prompt on the screen and you're ready to use EMAIL at once.

Figure 1.3. CompuServe's EMAIL.

London-based InfoLine provides a broad range of specialized technical and business information to thousands of corporate users in Great Britain and abroad, and has done so for about the last decade. Here is a search example drawn from their "Guide to Pergamon InfoLine." It demonstrates how database searching is conducted and will give the reader a feel for the increase in the level of complexity as one moves further into the command level (mentioned in the CompuServe example as a "shortcut" method, which means going directly into the database without using menus).

Searching. The command SELECT is used both to enter single search terms and to combine several terms linked by Boolean operators.

11.1 General Index Terms

A database record is divided into separate fields.

The information contained in each field is indexed and included in one or more separate indexes for searching.

For most databases, we create a General Index; this is usually the most frequently searched index and is made up of single items taken from "text" field such as the title, abstract, or descriptors. You should always consult the individual database reference manual to check what terms are included in the General Index.

Terms from the General Index of any database do not require an index prefix. An index prefix identifies the type of search term.

The SELECT command can be abbreviated to the single letter S. Synonymous commands are COMBINE and FIND.

The SELECT command may be used in the following ways:
a) To search for a single term, e.g.

S BICYCLE

In response to a SELECT command, a set is created; each set is numbered sequentially. The response to the above search statement is:

SET 1: 1470 BICYCLE

b) To search for a combination of terms, e.g.

S BICYCLE AND WHEEL

Boolean operators are used to relate terms in a logical manner. Boolean operators used on InfoLine are:

OR	Abbreviated to	O
ANd	Abbreviated to	A
ANd NOT	Abbreviated to	AN

A set is created for each term in your search statement as well as the result, e.g.

S IRON O STEEL

SET 1:	8694	IRON
SET 2:	10001	STEEL
SET 3:	17446	IRON OR STEEL

The "AND NOT" operator is used to remove concepts from your search strategy, e.g.

S FERROUS A N FERRIC

SET 1:	1876	FERROUS
SET 2:	817	FERRIC
SET 3:	1672	FERROUS A N FERRIC

By suitable use of parentheses and Boolean operators, fairly complex search strategies may be entered in one statement, e.g.

S (SILK O COTTON O WOOL) A (SHIRT O BLOUSE)

c) to combine previously created sets, e.g.

S 1 A 4

S (2 0 5) A SYNTHETIC

Figure 1.4. Pergamon InfoLine's general search terms.

COMPARISON

The above examples contrast the two main styles of working online, namely, menu-driven and command-driven. The difference is in the increased level of intellectual abstraction at the command level. The user must think about search logic, language, and plans instead of choosing from a "menu" of options. If CompuServe offered only the command level to its large public of users, much searching would slow down immediately and probably stop. Large mixed audiences aren't prepared for or interested in intense mental exercises as part of their online experience. Other better funded, better equipped, better educated, or more strongly motivated users may be able to cope with the command level, but that remains to be fully proved.

USING AN ONLINE SERVICE IS DIFFICULT

As the reader can see from the examples, online systems are not easy to use, nor are they idiot proof. On the other hand, they aren't bewildering even to those who are only somewhat familiar with terminals, computers, and Boolean logic operations. Yet, there are many in the online market who are confused by the operational complexity and mental abstractions involved, and, unfortunately, they are too easy for marketers to overlook or dismiss.

Efforts are underway to make operations easier and more attractive for everyone. On some systems the search commands and operator instructions can be entered in plain language, in plain language abbreviations, or, in some cases, by stroking specially designated keys on the keyboard. Many users rely on relatively easy-to-use multiple choice lists, the "Menus" and "Online Helps," which appear automatically on their screens. Still, printed operator reference manuals and less formally written user guides are needed for operating most systems.

CUSTOMERS

The diverse organizations and individuals who subscribe to and use online services range from universities and research centers, governments, and multinational industries to the doctor, lawyer, accountant, stock broker, businessman, computer buff, and local librarian—anyone, in fact, who works with data or information and has access to a computer might be a customer; anyone who uses timely data should be a customer.

GROWING SUCCESS

Automated support for knowledge work is a fixture of the Information age because the relatively quick market acceptance of online services laid enough of a solid foundation for the electronic publishing industry to grow quickly. The technology, marketing, and image building of the vendors, and to a lesser degree the efforts of paper publishers, have been the driving forces of the new industry.

In the last decade the industry has become strong enough to mount a growing challenge to the traditional perceptions and practices of knowledge work and to disturb the role of traditional knowledge institutions. This has been done by: rechanneling many of the new and traditional demands for manual information searches into online database searching by delivering a better cost/benefit ratio as well as freedom of time/place in searching; creating and offering complete, wide-ranging databases that attract and encourage formerly "impossible to do" searches; stimulating new and unprecedented levels of demand for timely information by brilliant applications of database, telecommunications, and computer technologies to information strategies, problems, and issues; and fitting smoothly and productively into the growing trends of computerization, service industrialization, organizational change, and the global expansion of markets.

INDUSTRY GROWTH

Industry revenues took off when the market got bigger. In some instances company equity has increased dramatically, thereby attracting new capital investment and stimulating new ventures. Three examples of solid growth in the United States are (1) if taken at its January 1987 share price of $32, the overall value of Telerate must approach $1½ billion (based on an estimated 50 million shares);[1] (2) in 1986 Quotron was sold to Citicorp for $680 million;[2] (3) Automatic Data Processing, a relative newcomer in the financial field, currently has 55,000 quotation terminals and 7,000 microcomputer-based work stations in use, the two activities together accounting for about 25 percent of its $1.2 billion in total revenues from all sources.[3]

EXAMPLES OF SUBSCRIBER BASES AND REVENUES

On the whole, the online industry world-wide is not a huge industry at the end of its first twenty years, currently probably not more than

$2 billion in total revenue per year, but the evidence of accomplishment is there in growing equity and revenue, growth rates, earnings, size of the various organizations, and the quality, range, and types of online services and electronic databases. Below is a comparison of the earnings and size of some of the leading United States and British online service vendors. It has been said of the industry that in "1982 total industry revenue was approximately $1.2 billions—it is estimated at $10 billion by 1990."[4]

1.2. Computers
TELETYPEWRITERS

The common terminal device that works with a mainframe computer directly is the teletypewriter. It usually has no screen and all of its transactions, conducted at the command level of the system, are printed out on paper. For a computer to be used in its place the computer must behave like a teletypewriter and talk with its voice. Two pieces of extra equipment for a computer allow it to operate in a terminal mode, namely, the modem and the control program called *terminal emulation software*. (These are discussed below.)

MICROCOMPUTER SYSTEMS[6]

"A microcomputer is a computer processor contained in a single integrated circuit." A computer is "an electronic device for performing predefined computation at high speed and with great accuracy." A computer system is the computer and everything it takes to make it work, including software, the components that control the behavior of the computer. To make a microcomputer do an online search, software called terminal emulation software is usually required. It causes the microcomputer to behave like a teletypewriter.

MODEM[7]

As you read this passage many subscribers to online systems are using a microcomputer equipped with a modem to go online with a vendor's mainframe computer. The modem is the essential element in that process because it allows the two computers to transmit data back and forth over telephone lines. In the late 1980's it is still necessary for impulses traveling over telephone lines to be transmitted in tones.

SERVICE	SUBSCRIBERS 1985	$ REVENUES 1984
		9.5
Compuserve*	260,000	(Millions)
Dow Jones**	235,000	39.0
Lexis/Nexis/Medis	180,000	125.0
Dialcom [electronic mail]	150,000	874.0
Financial Info. Serv.	76,665	175.0
Dialog	70,000	59.0
Monitor (Reuters)	65,000	310.0
The Source***	60,000	11.7
Financial Control Serv.	35,485	60.0
Bunker Ramo Info Serv.	31,500	62.1
Telerate	30,000	114.0
BRS (Thyssen-Bornemisza)	26,000	10.0
Dunsprint	24,179	63.0
Viewtron	15,000	n/a
Newsnet	11,000	n/a
Commodity News Serv.	10,000	40.0
OCLC	7,483	37.0
Sharp APL	6,700	9.5
Mark III	6,000	8.0
Vu/Text Info. Serv.	2,360	n/a

1987 Subscriber Bases: *380,000, **320,000, ***80,000. Source: *New York Times.*[5]

Figure 1.5. The revenues of twenty United States and British electronic publishers, listed by size of subscriber bases.

The pitch of the tones is changed to represent the information. Most microcomputers do not automatically emit tones suitable for this purpose. The modem is a device wired between the microcomputer and the home or office telephone that converts (changes in pitch, modulates) the serial information of the microcomputer into tones suitable for telephone transmission. Modem stands for MOdulator/ DEModulator.

TERMINAL SOFTWARE[8]

Most modems can be operated either by direct commands with predefined functions, like "AT X2 DT 9 (408) 767–2676" (which commands the modem to follow a special protocol to dial the phone number of another computer in the 408 area code), or they can be commanded by menus provided by the terminal emulation software inserted or installed in the microcomputer. After inserting the number to be called in the computer's memory, the menu user can then choose "Dial" from the menu on his screen and the call will be placed automatically. Many users rely on software because it serves as an easy-to-use intermediary between the user and the command complexity of the modem.

ONCE ONLINE

By using either a teletypewriter or a computer with the terminal emulation software inserted and the modem set, a user can call the vendor's mainframe and go online to search hundreds of databases: he can send messages, leave messages, receive messages, chat online with other users, or transfer files with and to other computers; do banking and financial transactions of all kinds, get stock quotations and a wide range of other financial data, shop, or swap; obtain copies of public domain software (only computers can do this); make airline, hotel, and restaurant reservations; consult an encyclopedia; check the latest weather and news reports; plan a flight; play games; gossip; and many other trivial or important activities.[9]

EFFECT

In January 1986, a study conducted by the Electronic Industries Association determined that 15 percent of all American households had a personal computer. Millions more are in use in public and private institutions in the United States. Given all the terminals, microcomputers, and modems in the United States and Great Britain, there is now an access-equipped population numbering in the millions, a small percentage of whom have already been instructed in the techniques of online activities and are users. The numbers and types of databases, services, and knowledge products are growing to meet the estimated demand because the equipment that makes it reasonable to do so is fully developed and widely distributed and the number of individuals instructed in its use is growing. "The explosion in United States electronic databases, and usage, is almost breathtaking."[10] If the explosion was sparked by intensive product development and marketing activities, it is fueled by the current widespread use of microcomputer systems.

1.3. An Introduction to Pricing, Marketing, and Selling in the Online Industry

NO LONGER NOVEL

The vendors had the unique opportunity (and the very hard marketing job) of introducing automation into knowledge work in the private sector; they named it, priced it, explained it, operated the systems and sold the idea and services to large audiences of knowledge workers, and then instructed them on their databases and systems. They developed and applied hardware and software solutions to many of the problems they encountered, solutions they then rented or sold as needed. Online searching isn't a new idea anymore, and as a true mark of their success it is now taken for granted like office photocopying, smart cards, local area networks, microcomputing, or dozens of other recent successful high tech innovations in knowledge systems and communications. Through its acceptance, growth, and technical accomplishment it is becoming very different in its ambition, potential scope, economics, politics, staff, and operations from any other type of knowledge institution found in academia, paper publishing, or electronic communications.

THE NUMBER ONE MARKETING ISSUE

In business and banking, health care, and information science, for example, hundreds of interrelated databases are online in the United States and Great Britain. Here is a random sampling of a few topic areas and a rough count of how many databases are readily identifiable for each subject in the United States: computer software (85), legislative and regulatory information (35), new venture planning (22), energy (15), agriculture (10), social sciences information (8), petroleum industry (7), humanities (4), United Nations information (2), Japan (2). These are but a few of the several thousand databases available online in the United States, more than 2,200 by one count. The issue is obvious: how is the impatient, ever more cost-and-service-conscious buyer moved to choose among the well-positioned, heavily marketed online systems and databases available, and what can be done to steer his or her choices?

CHANGING INDUSTRY ENVIRONMENT

The industry is showing the early symptoms of maturity. Growth increasingly eludes even the most successful online organizations.

On the one hand some companies are gaining in market strength; mergers and equity growth, while publisher and major customer re-alignments have greatly increased the marketing clout of some online organizations. On the other hand, other companies have plateaued, regressed, or gone under, particularly several noteworthy new ventures by major participants. Today, all ventures, but particularly new ones, attract effective competition.

Price increases to existing customers are more difficult to pull off and riskier than before. The other growth options—increasing customer use in markets where customers pay use charges, growing market share in markets where customers pay yearly fees, and both activities in markets where customers are charged both ways simultaneously—are becoming important marketing activities. Also, the mission of selling more accounts to increase market share frequently has to be accomplished in the less lucrative and more difficult markets. Taken together, these conditions increase the need for marketing creativity and efficiency.

A ZEROTH LAW OF ONLINE MARKETING

In thermodynamics and even in robotics the three fundamental laws have been enhanced by the addition of a Zeroth law, which should have come first but was discovered later and promoted ahead of the first law. I nominate *Pricing determines marketing strategy* as a candidate for the Zeroth law of online marketing. It meets the test for a law, namely, it always happens under the circumstances.

The arguments underlying the Zeroth law are discussed in detail in chapter 2, starting with section 2:1. Let it suffice for now to say that there are three pricing schemes:

(1) Annual fees scheme. The customer pays a yearly total fee that covers all use of the system. The marketing consequence of choosing the annual fee is that marketing has a homogeneous mission—to market to an all-buyer market.

(2) Use fee scheme. No annual fee is paid, but the customer pays charges for each use occasion. The marketing consequence of choosing a use fee is that marketing has a homogeneous mission—to market to an all-user market.

(3) Mixed pricing scheme. There is a combination of fixed fees and use charges for each customer. The marketing consequence of choosing mixed pricing is that marketing has a heterogeneous mission: first, to market to all buyers and, second, to market

to all users, in that specific 1—2 order. Mixed pricing is used by most online firms, so most marketing in the electronic publishing industry is heterogeneous.

THE NEED FOR PROACTIVE MARKETING

When pricing that targets the user as a source of revenue is chosen another kind of selling becomes important, namely, how to influence the user who has the seller's database (or even several other databases) to choose to use the seller's database in a specific situation, and to choose to use it often. Proactive marketing addresses this issue directly, along with the issue of getting initial buyers signed up for services. In both kinds of sales the normal sales fundamentals apply, but there are some unusual wrinkles.

The quality-cost-service triad retains its traditional importance with buyers. Creatively presented benefits, the value-added characteristics of a service or product, which relate the elements of the triad to the buyer's perceived information needs and hoped-for productivity, may be foremost among the deciding factors for sales below the high price threshold. Buyer attitudes about modernness, high tech, and investments in knowledge itself can also be factors. Selling above the high price threshold in today's high tech climate requires a formal proposal, contracting, and a sales management process that is so lengthy and complex that is is almost always handled by a sales team under the direction of a senior sales or corporate executive.

In either sale fewer buyers can afford to compare 100 or even ten databases, and few, if any, will need, will want, or can afford all of those available. Choices have to be made. At most the average buyer might be able to compare a few likely condidates. The ones chosen for final consideration might well be those that have advertised widely or are known to the buyer by some other marketing communication such as user feedback, a colleague's recommendation, association sponsorship, magazine or newsletter articles, trade shows, or even direct mail. Proactive, imaginative marketing communications make the difference in getting a specific online service or its products either on the buyer's short list for final consideration or for actual use at the terminal.

PRICE RANGES

After the reader is acquainted with the industry, he or she may wish to study the detailed and complex pricing schedules of many services.

For introductory purposes, let's keep our observations general: hourly service charges and connect fees range from a low of tens of dollars and pounds per use unit, up to hundreds of dollars and pounds per use unit, depending on a host of price and charging scheme variables pegged to databases and use patterns. Fixed yearly fees can range from a low of thousands of dollars and pounds per annual contract on up, depending on the same variables mentioned above and on what the market will bear.

COST/BENEFIT ISSUES

It is important to understand that not all pricing in the online industry is rational or customer centered. When users are confronted with ten different databases in one online knowledge product, each with different pricing, and with each pricing structure also different, they can be daunted and perplexed. Often users will search the database, hoping for the best. When the bill comes, they may choose not to use the database again unless they can pass on the charges to another payer. (Users can be alienated from the vendor's best products for no other reason than the failure to standardize the industry's pricing and database structures.) When users understand pricing, they can modify searching techniques to manage cost, but this is not seen as being totally in the best interest of the vendor's pockets.

At the present time users are often expected to invest time and energy to learn such operational strings as: (1) the unique searching features of each database; (2) the pricing structure of each database; (3) how to estimate the actual price of the search as a whole; and (4) clever strategies for risk management in searching to keep costs within the brackets of their ability to pay, on the one hand, and their perceived value of the information, on the other.

NO-COST/BENEFIT ISSUES

Another cost/benefit issue is raised by the advocates of the school of thought that holds that all information is a public utility and that selling it introduces a barrier that denies access to most people. Western societies, they point out, have a tradition of free access to information that supports this argument: enormous amounts of free or very low cost information can be obtained through publicly supported libraries and study centers, schools, universities, research centers, radio and television, and governmental publishing and outreach organizations at all levels.

A twin tradition of free information is maintained by the privately sponsored activities of private universities and schools, corporations and businesses, religious institutions, foundations, learned societies, clubs, and civic organizations, and even some wealthy individuals. The intellectual and economic benefits of wide access to information to a free society are incalculable. Together these two traditions form one of the major safeguards of our intellectural freedoms. Online services, they argue, should fit within or support this tradition.

THE PROPRIETARY INFORMATION TRADITION

There is a strong tradition of timely proprietary information available only to those who can and will pay for it. That the restricted distribution of information works for the benefit of a free society is indisputable: contract research is the most powerful example there is of that benefit; patents, copyrights, and stock market quotes are but a few among many others. It is in the manner of this branch of the information tradition that most online systems do business. Part of it comes from the fact that much of the data and information available online are copyrighted and that royalties are paid for their use. Another aspect is the timeliness in which online systems excel, and hot information is worth a premium to someone somewhere because it is an advantage in the conducting of human affairs and business.

This boils down to a single dispute, namely, as more and more databases come online, the benefits of electronic searching are open only to the few; the many are left with the traditional manual techniques to do the same job. Business reality intrudes at this point. If the vendors are to continue to provide the systems and services they do, they have to make money. If they don't, their capital will migrate to industries where there is a return on investment. This economic law, if that is what it is, determines that electronic publishing will seek out and serve best those markets where there is an expectation of profit.

ONLINE CHARGES

There are hundreds of free computerized bulletin boards and message systems in the private sector. Online databases in the private sector are not free however. The only real limit on user searching is cost/benefit perception and the ability to pay. The user must consider the cost of membership fees, connect charges, and any other online fees the user would have to pay to the vendor (plus his out-of-pocket expenses for his time, the microcomputer system, modem, and terminal emulation software and telephone bills). These charges can be substantial (depending on user and pricing variables).

The issue of how much to charge (and how to rationalize charges) is one of the problems in the industry. The issue persists as a negative result of disjointed actions on pricing and database construction by the database producers. (Databases are often produced by organizations such as learned societies or paper publishers who are not the marketers of their own electronic products.) Because of the effect of pricing actions and other restrictions and convenants initiated by the producers, vendors do not have a free hand in pricing, marketing, and creating knowledge products responsive to enduser or market realities. (These conflicts are not a one-way street, however; producers have important points on their side of the story too, as well as some legitimate complaints about the actions of online vendors). Even if these problems disappeared tomorrow, vendors would still have to charge for their services, but pricing could be rationalized.

ISSUES IN CHARGING

From the vendor's side the failings of the database producers lie in two areas: product creation and royalty charges. No standard exists for product creation, for a systematic technical arrangement of all the databases. Royalty charges are all over the map and are not necessarily related to market values because they are, for the most part, functions of traditions and activities in the paper publishing industry, or vanity charges imposed by a producer organization that is deeply impressed with itself. When the vendor bundles databases from different producers to make an online knowledge product, each database in the product still retains its own unique organization, pricing, and searching protocols.

A professional archival expert can probably master the databases in a single area of knowledge, but few average users have the need, patience, training, or funds for doing so. This barrier to seamless use disturbs buyer and user satisfaction and productivity because the benefits of the product are hard to obtain at a known price. Vendor revenues are affected, of course, as are the earnings of the database producers.

PRODUCT QUALITY

Imagine how it might have been if the first generation of vendors had taken the approach that the publisher's tapes were industrial waste, by-products to be unloaded. Today's vendor might be the electronic publishing equivalent of the paper publisher's discount outlet. Instead, even where they weren't publisher dominated, vendors positioned their businesses on quality information. This was good business, as it turned out. When the boom in use came, vendors were soon telling their story through large sales forces and extensive advertising and marketing campaigns to keep their established markets growing, to keep the demand for services growing, and to increase their subscriber base and market share.

Effective competition sprang up for certain lucrative markets (and even in some not so lucrative ones). Electronic publishers have continued to position electronic databases as quality products in the minds of their prospects throughout the history of the industry. When higher revenues have to be obtained to cover the costs of growth, competition, and marketing communications, the image of quality pays off, because high quality and high price are intuitively related in most markets.

1.4. Our Societal and Institutional Environments Are Changing and Online Services Are Playing A Role in Some of the Changes

THE RISE OF SERVICE-DOMINATED ECONOMIES

The United States and British economies are dominated by service industries. Economic dependence and military and social importance put a premium on the quality and productivity of knowledge work. Our current business and governmental setup consumes more data and information than any economic and social system in history. Survival and continued national success seems to hang on the quantity and quality of timely intelligence activities, business and governmental communications, and knowledge work in all sectors of society.

COMMUNICATION TRIAGE

These particular societal and economic drivers encourage, demand, and reward a high level of personal mastery and participation in information processes; they also foster awareness of, use of, careers in, and dependence on them. Young people are intensively trained to respond to information imperatives. The more they respond, the greater their rewards. Those who can't or won't are shunted to one side, victims of communication triage. Keeping up is a problem for all. The jobs currently being created in the United States and Great Britain seem to be mainly for skilled knowledge workers and younger unskilled laborers according to recent United States and British studies of long-term employment trends. This situation is on its way to becoming the permanent context of both childhood and adult life.

KNOWLEDGE INSTITUTIONS

This evolution is changing the roles and operations of knowledge institutions. For example, the library, the most venerable of knowledge institutions, is changing because knowledge work itself is changing and decentralizing. These issues have prompted renewal efforts and new service experiments such as the kiosklike decentralized library stations at Bell Laboratories in the United States. Bell is trying to move the library to the knowledge worker by establishing a "branch bank" system that includes both human and automated "tellers." These tellers are placed near cafeterias and other gathering points for easy consultation.

This scheme is a an effort to keep in touch with the needs and perceptions of the knowledge worker. To not try something new is to risk being cut out of the knowledge loop by managerial attitudes toward fixed costs, changing organizational and behavioral styles, and the rapid deployment of online systems accessed through the AT&T microcomputers sitting on every desk at Bell Labs.

KNOWLEDGE WORK IS CHANGING

The library may not be called on to do the same work it used to do for managers because of the spread of online systems in the corporate suite and the changing roles of management: "We are shifting the ideal of the model employee from one who carries out orders correctly to one who takes responsibility and initiative, monitors his or her own work, and uses managers and supervisors in their new role of facilitators, teachers and consultants."[11] Less library support may be needed for these managers, and the directness of online systems may have an increased appeal and application because there is less to be done, and it can be done online more quickly and conveniently.

THE STRESS OF CHANGE

Librarians point out that their studies show that information searches done outside the library can be incomplete, may be misleading in their results, and may not adequately inform either management or knowledge workers.[12] The author has been told however of the advanced conclusions of a study by a United States online vendor, still being written as this book is going to press, that claims to have determined that online searching by professionals is more effective and efficient than online searching by librarians (in a valid test of comparable searches on pertinent professional topics). Judgment must be reserved, but findings such as these, if valid, would extend the work demonstrating superior online search efficiency by Muller and Wilson[13] cited in the next section. Clearly, the librarians have a point, and the unresolved controversy is mentioned as one example of the stresses that changing work and information patterns are introducing into lives of knowledge institutions, managers, and knowledge workers.

This debate aside, the idea and use of online systems for information gathering is slowly spreading among all sectors of knowledge work and management, according to computer industry survey studies. In the long run every knowledge worker and manager may have to know how to search properly and accurately and have personal access to online systems. Who knows what this will mean to centralized libraries?

ORGANIZATIONAL PATTERNS

In the United States the days of the "top-down, captain-of-industry" style management may be ending, and this may bode well indeed for online systems: "The shift to knowledge work as the new center of gravity of the work force will altogether force the United States to rethink the traditional organizational structure. . . . America's shift to an information based economy has precipitated the emergence of a whole new management style."[14]

As flatter, leaner, and, presumably, more competitive organizations have developed, and as acceptable dual career ladders for knowledge workers are implemented, online databases may be increasingly important to individual and organizational success. The strongest reason is their estimated productivity. Muller and Wilson report online searches that were 21 percent faster than comparable manual searches and 24 percent cheaper.[15] Productivity gains mean a lot. They demonstrate that online searching makes the process of slimming down more feasible. Another reason is that online searching by managers can feed decision-making and competitive information directly to knowledge workers and management peers when it is needed, anytime, anywhere: "In knowledge-based organizations knowledge workers are the 'bosses' and the 'manager' is in a supporting role as their planner and coordinator. . . . The small team and cross disciplinary team heads the list (of organizational formats) of these new structures [in the American corporation]."[16]

Small structures seem to fit the pattern of change partly because they are cost efficient in gathering and assessing information and, one assumes, tend to be decisive in its use. Also, they are viewed favorably because today's knowledge workers work differently than their counterparts in the 1970's did: "the work style of the information worker in a two-career family is flexible scheduling—job-sharing, flextime, and part-time—and flexible benefits."[17] Under these conditions online databases are almost ideal for many research activities, business transactions, electronic mail, decision-making support, and other essential communication and information activities. If work is becoming a distributed, relatively unsupervisable activity, hinged on individual responsibility and time management, a portable, highly flexible "electronic office" complete with database access is a key tool.

ONLINE FITS IN WELL

The above model of organizational change should be read as an extreme position rather than the middle ground for all knowledge, industrial, or governmental organizations in the United States. No one knows for sure the extent of these changes, and many observers have an ax to grind for or against these changes and trends. Still, if online services can be expected to fit well on the organizational extreme, their future growth and use is assured because they fit well in conventional organizations. On the whole, online services seem to be well positioned for flexibly serving the emerging economic, psychological, organizational, spatial, and technical needs of the knowledge market.

PRIVATE AND PUBLIC SECTOR COMPETITION

There is competition between the profit-making private sector online services and government and nonprofit online services that are operating with a free information philosophy. In the current political and economic climate in the United States and Great Britain, many of the free information organizations are finding that charging something for their information is the only practical way to continue to provide it. Many of these databases are now carried successfully by "commercial" vendors to their much wider user audiences. The revenues generated help keep these databases going.

The reader will have to resolve this issue for himself, but he should keep in mind the economic realities and take up the question of whether goverment and nonprofit institutions should be using their scarce resources to compete with private resources in an area where national needs are being met and where most of the same information is still accessible to almost everyone by manual means.

Notes

1. "Dow Jones Agrees to Buy Telerate Stake for $133.1 Million," *Wall Street Journal* 1, no. 19 (1987).
2. "Automatic Data Get Merrill Lynch Work for a Quote System," *Wall Street Journal* 1, no. 14 (1987).
3. Ibid.
4. P. Taylor, "An Explosion of New Databases," *Financial Times* 1, no. 10 (1986).
5. Ibid. and A. Pollack, "Ruling May Not Aid Videotext," *New York Times*, September 15, 1987.
6. *Apple® Personal Modem User's Manual* (Cupertino, 1985), glossary.
7. Ibid.
8. Ibid.
9. For further information on these issues see R. E. Hoover, "The Executive's Guide to Online Information Services" (White Plains: Knowledge Industries, 1984), 1–47.
10. "Automatic Data."
11. J. Naisbitt and P. Aburdene, "Reinventing the Corporation," *Chief Executive*, Autumn 1985, 40–41.
12. R. Basch, "The Electronic Client: User Expectations and Searcher Responsibilities." Medford: *Proceedings–1986*, National Online Meeting: Learned Information: (1986): 19–26.
13. P. Muller and R. Wilson, *Pricing Policies for Parallel Publishing* (Oxford: Elsevier, 1985), 1, 29.
14. Naisbitt and Aburdene, "Reinventing the Corporation."
15. Muller and Wilson, *Pricing Policies.*
16. Naisbitt and Aburdene, "Reinventing the Corporation."
17. Ibid.

2
ONLINE MARKETING IN A WORKING PERSPECTIVE

2.1. The Information Environment

All of the marketing plans of the online industry are enacted in the domain of the information system. As shown in figure 2.1, the information system supplies the endconsumer from its electronic and manual archives.

On some occasions the endconsumer consults the original sources and events directly (e.g., stock quotes), but more often research findings and other data are compiled from all relevant sources (by either a user or an enduser) and then transformed by an enduser into value added information. The information is packaged by the enduser into an appropriate communications format for the endconsumer and then is delivered. See figure 2.2.

The endconsumer's motivation drives the information system, but the enduser determines what the endconsumer will get from the manual and electronic searches of the users. Marketing complications arise from the unclear roles that any of these people may play at any

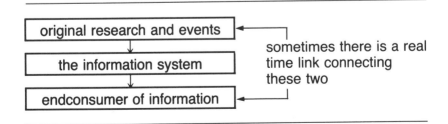

Figure 2.1.   The information system.

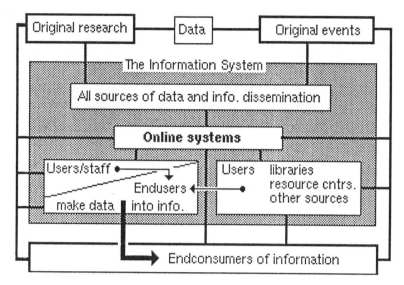

Figure 2.2. The functions of the information system.

given moment. For example, the endconsumer may be an enduser or even a user of an online system, and, sometimes, he may be a contributor to the databases; the enduser may also be a user of an online system and, sometimes, even a contributor to the databases; the user uses the keyboard of the online system and reports the output of his searches; rarely is a user found in one of the other roles.

Let's look closely at the enduser as he is shown in the lower-left-hand quadrant of figure 2.2. The information system is focused by the enduser for the endconsumer. The enduser chooses for the endconsumer. When he selects material gathered by a user for inclusion in his final report to the endconsumer, that particular piece of material becomes "useful information" deemed valuable to the world just by the selection that has been made. *The difference is between potential value and actual value.* Before a unit of material is chosen for inclusion in a final endconsumer report, its value is potential; after the choice has been made, the value is actual. The enduser is shown in the diagram supported by two populations of users, those on his personal staff and those on the staff of knowledge institutions patronized by the enduser or by other users on his staff. Collectively, users have been viewed by marketing and online management as the "customers" for online services, but an expanded view suggests strongly that it is the enduser or the endconsumer who is really the actor defined as the traditional customer.

2:2. The Pricing Muddle and Its Effect on Marketing

Ever since the first person went online, pricing in the online industry has been a major problem, especially for customers and marketers. There are hostile marketing, management, information provider, and customer camps fighting over every issue from flat fees to price elasticity. No one has been able to establish industry policies and standards that improve the situation and are profitable, acceptable, and productive for all. The result is an ongoing pricing muddle that considerably complicates marketing.

Two pricing issues will be examined here: (1) the structure of pricing and its profound influence on marketing and selling practices; and (2) how the pricing muddle came about and is perpetuated.

THE NATURE OF ONLINE SERVICE CHARGES

There are two ways of charging for online services in the online industry:

(1) Fixed charges: sign-up fees, monthly minimums, monthly subscription charges, installation charges, charges for manuals, etc.
(2) Variable charges: charges for each minute of online use (sometimes variable by baud rate), charges for each line of printing or document delivery, charges based on parts of the document viewed (such as title, source, abstract, or full text), charges by search, etc. These vary in their total value by the combined costs of specific user choices and activities.

There are many combinations of fixed and variable charges in use—almost as many as there are online organizations. Charges can be inconsistent within the same service. Online organizations struggle with the structure of their pricing as much or more than they do with the levels of their charges. Rates are often presented to the buyer in a complicated format, and buyers subject to variable charges have no real way of estimating or predicting actual total costs. Online services spend an inordinate percentage of total resources designing, revising, and maintaining billing programs that work and are accurate. And, as one wit has observed, some statistician ought to look for a correlation between system crashes and billing runs.

EFFECT OF PRICING ON MARKETING

Pricing can be arrayed on a continuum with fixed price schemes at one end and variable price schemes at the other. At one end appear all of the fixed price schemes: there is no charge for variable use; instead, buyers pay a flat fee for the whole year, or pay a large "sign up" fee, or pay a fixed monthly fee. There is no limit on the amount or type of use. At the opposite end appear all of the variable schemes: the buyer pays nothing up front but is charged for his system use each time he uses it in a specific mode, with the rate established by either the minute, the nature of the data retrieved, the search, or some combination of these or other methods. The pricing continuum is shown in figure 2.3.

A ZEROTH LAW: PRICING DETERMINES MARKETING STRATEGY

When all of the seller's revenue is generated by a fixed commitment from the buyer, marketing's resources will be used identifying initial buyers, qualifying them, and selling them. Each sale made to the initial buyer is essentially complete when the contract is signed. Follow-up marketing tactics to reduce buyer cancellations and to stimulate prompt renewal when contract periods are up are not part of the initial sale per se, but are addressed to the same set of buyers and will use many of the same appeals and techniques of the initial sale.

When all of the seller's revenue is generated by a variable scheme, the seller sends user identification numbers to everyone who is a qualified prospective buyer or user. After the ID numbers are distributed, marketing spends its time and resources convincing the buyer to consult the system's databases over and over. From the

Figure 2.3. The pricing continuum of the online industry.

seller's point of view the second sale is never "completed" or "closed" the way the initial sale is. The second sale continues to require marketing attention, expense, and effort (see figure 2.4).

The seller concentrates his energies, creativity, resources, marketing communications, and marketing intelligence on one type of buyer and one type of sale. Marketing is both driven and focused by pricing with its maximum effort going into overcoming the price resistance of the targeted buyers and in mastering the marketing and sales situation.

If opting for a pricing scheme anywhere on the continuum automatically determines marketing, what happens if one chooses the middle? Choices along the middle entail different marketing consequences than those on the extremes because marketing and sales complexity automatically doubles. Most of the online industry instinctively, and perhaps unconsciously, prices its products and services along the middle of the continuum by opting for a mix of fixed and variable pricing. At first glance mixed pricing is desirable. It thins out some buyer objections to pricing levels in both types of sales by lowering both price thresholds simultaneously, as depicted in figure 2.5. Lower price resistance across the board should mean more revenue from all sources and a larger market share.

The marketing reality is different than expected or predicted. What is not obvious is that to get the desired revenue and market share the seller must be truly market driven; have *superb* marketing leadership, discipline, and drive; possess extensive human and financial resources; and have abundant creativity, marketing imagi-

	FIXED PRICING	VARIABLE PRICING
INITIAL SALE	**HEAVY EFFORT TO SUPPORT A DIFFICULT BUYING DECISION BY THE INITIAL BUYER**	LIGHT EFFORT TO SUPPORT THE BUYING DECISION
SECOND SALE	LIGHT EFFORT TO SUPPORT THE BUYING DECISION	**HEAVY EFFORT TO SUPPORT A DIFFICULT BUYING DECISION BY THE USER ON EACH USE OCCASION**

Figure 2.4. The effect of pricing on sales effort.

nation, marketing research, customer intelligence, and tactical excellence. All of these "must" factors have to be present and fully functional for the seller to succeed at repeatedly making both the first and second sales. Effort and complexity must also be taken into account: marketing must mount twice the overall effort against an underestimated probability of failure, and the first and second sales are so totally different in their planning, nature, complexity, and requirements as to be almost incompatible in the same marketing and selling organization.

Rather than viewing mixed pricing as reducing market resistance to both sales, after taking the factors mentioned above into account, management should recognize it as leaving in place an unknown degree of price resistance to both sales. Also, marketing has to deal with the problem of having only half of the human and financial resources that would be available if either of the other two schemes has been chosen. The danger is that the firm won't be competitive enough. The alternative is to double the resources for the marketing plan. In all of these discussions there is the sobering management reality that most marketing and selling organizations have their hands full selling well in one concentrated market style, not to mention funding, developing, perfecting, managing, and executing two incompatible ones.

Management should weigh the effect that pricing has on overall sales and marketing performance, decisions related to managing and staffing the sales organization, the cost and complexity of billing and customer communications about pricing, and the wide-ranging sales

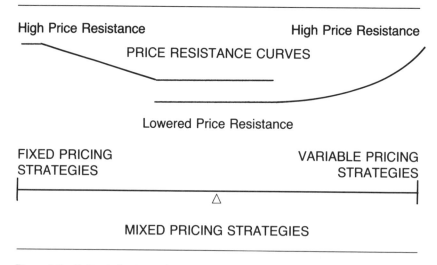

Figure 2.5. Estimated price resistance.

tactics required. Marketing and sales managers distrust dilution of marketing effort. They resist being rendered helpless by decisions from on high that they can't influence with their market expertise and insight. Marketing managers say privately that some online organizations do not permit them to participate in pricing decisions, even though the decision being made determines what marketing and sales will do in the market. The irony is twofold because shockingly few senior online executives make sales calls or meet often with buyers and users, while marketing is the best informed company unit on the market's attitudes about current and future pricing.

This whole pricing/marketing situation must be consciously reconsidered if the muddle is to be rationalized. Additional considerations such as whether or not the service is new and first in a market that it can hope to dominate, what percentage of the market (by user and amount of use) already belongs to the company or the competition, and what the marketer's goals are, are but a few of the variables which have to be factored into a set of rationalized pricing decisions. These considerations are uncomfortably complex, buyer-and-competition centered and interrelated, especially in high tech markets.

In this pricing and marketing environment the long-term goals of the marketing organization and the productivity goals for the service should be as definite as is humanly possible. Top management must recognize that it too is bound by the limitations imposed by the interrelatedness of these factors. Changing strategic pricing and sales goals later on is not as simple as ordering the marketing/sales organization to produce more revenue from the many shallow pockets of users, and less revenue from the few deep pockets of new buyers. To respond to that order, the whole marketing, order entry, and accounting system would have to be retooled and retrained from top to bottom, and consideration given to the very serious and delicate problem of selling the new pricing to current users. A host of complex attitudinal and motivational adjustments must be attempted, and staffing, compensation, and other human factors must be sorted out. These are expensive and time-consuming back-office changes which disrupt, distract, and impair the marketing and selling organization and, perhaps, the user of the system for long periods of time—time that the competition may use all too well.

2.3. Online Selling is a Multistep Process When Mixed Pricing Is Widely Used

Since most online organizations charge for their services and products using a mix of fixed and variable pricing, they face a two-step decision-making process in sales. The first buying decision, the initial sale, is a one-time event and it culminates in a formal agreement. It usually occurs at the instigation of the seller near the end of a persuasive marketing and selling process. The second buying decision happens later, after the installation of the system is completed. It is made every time a user goes online to search or when an enduser places an order for an online search. The marketing goal of the second sale is to cause the customer to *cycle* productively in place, coming back to use the system over and over with increasing frequency. Therefore the second sale is made at the instigation of the user, enduser, or the endconsumer of information. It happens after the initial sale is made, the system installed, the user has been instructed in its use, the user has appreciated, assimilated, internalized, and integrated the benefits of the service, and the user has figured out pricing to a workable extent.

2.4. There Are Many Differences Between the First and Second Sale that Affect Marketing

Thoughtful online marketing differentiates sharply between the tactical requirements for supporting the first and second sales programs because they are so different to both the seller and the buyer. Successful marketing tactics in both sales have to be tied directly to the buyer's relationship to the service and his responses to pricing. Edward Gottsman, former vice president of strategy at Mead Data Central, says, "The first purchase decision is made when the salesperson tries to convince the prospect to install the service. . . . This is a buying decision. . . . The potential customer still has to be persuaded that it's worth the effort to learn how to use the service and that the transaction charges to be paid when and if the service is used will not be too high."[1]

An examination of the differences between the initial and the second sale shows why marketing and selling for each sale must be different. A comparison of the differences also demonstrates why a single marketing communication strategy cannot encompass both the first and second sale in a focused, striking, motivating, and persuasive manner:

1ST SALE   The seller must capture and hold the attention of the buyer.

2D SALE   The user must ultimately respond to the system itself which will, in turn, hold his attention.

1ST SALE   The buyer might not be the user of the system. He may be cost oriented, analytical, and abstract, not in any way operational in his purchase analysis. The frame of reference used in evaluating the buying decision may extend far beyond the walls of the buying organization and its personalities.

2D SALE   The user of the system may have little or nothing to do with paying the bills but a lot to do with monitoring the charges. The decision-making frame of reference of the user is non-financial and organizationally bound for the most part.

1ST SALE   The seller knows when the sale is made because the buyer agrees to have the service installed and concludes a formal agreement.

2D SALE   From the seller's point of view, "use" is always a "sale" in the process of being made. Of necessity it remains "open" and "unconcluded" until the user returns again to use the service. It is always subject to further marketing influences.

1ST SALE   The technical effectiveness of the system is almost irrelevant to the buyer. Productivity versus cost is important.

2D SALE   The measure of effectiveness for the user is the time he saves for himself, which is much more important to him than abstract issues of productivity and price.

1ST SALE   The buyer's interest may be in the database holdings, overall intellectual productivity, and similar intellectual issues. For example, a key element in the decision may be an anticipated increase in research scope.

2D SALE   To the user the operational features of the system are, in a sense, of paramount importance. The way in which the system feeds research and data into a project or the organization as a whole may be an *abstraction* to many users and irrelevant to their mind set.

1ST SALE   The buyer will always have time-bound needs that influence the timing of his decision-making process. The decisions to buy, use, and pay must be made in accord with the timing of the buying organization's staffing, operations, sales, and budgeting cycles.

2D SALE   The user has a task mentality and isn't concerned with interlocking timing issues within the organization because he's usually not responsible for more than his tasks.

1ST SALE. The addition of automated research systems to the buying organization will not add to the personal prestige of the buyer.

2D SALE The user grows in personal status by being the active agent in the automation of data collection and research. He learns more about his work because of his searches and has increased power to find and retrieve materials for others. He controls the automated systems and uses them to produce benefits.

1ST SALE The buyer is located and identified by the proactivity of the seller. Also, the same buyer may be the designator of the users of the system.

2D SALE The user is often appointed or nominated by the buyer of the system. Users are then sought out, instructed, and cultivated by the seller especially in situations where the new service is merely one of many serving an organization.

1ST SALE After the sale is made the buyer requires little or no after sale support. He moves on to other issues.

2D SALE The user has substantial needs for after sale support from the seller's organization. The seller's instruction department, hotline, and telemarketing groups may be in frequent advisory and tutorial contact with the user after installation and start-up occurs.

1ST SALE The buyer has little contact with the seller and the system after installation, except for user feedback, advertising, and, perhaps, billing (unless he's a user too).

2D SALE The user has frequent contact with the marketing, operational, instructional, and technical materials offered, provided, and produced by the seller and forms revised impressions of the seller through these activities.

1ST SALE After its installation, the system often makes only a slight continuing impression on the buyer.

2D SALE The operational characteristics of the system make a powerful lasting impression on the user by changing his behavior, relationships, and work life. Judgments are formed quickly about the systems, the company, and its databases. Enhancements to the system play a large role in reinforcing, tempering, and adjusting these impressions.

Clearly, the first and second sale buyers and the sales them-selves differ sharply from each other. They cannot be successfully approached from the same marketing and sales viewpoint, even for the same product.

2.5. Marketing Has an Ombudsmanlike Obligation to Represent the Users' Interests In the Online Organization

In most online organizations the marketing department and the product development group are at opposite ends of the building, or even opposite ends of the earth. But they need to consider jointly a number of problems affecting the whole enterprise. For example, online systems are not idiot proof. Users get tangled up in them. The negative feelings created by these experiences feed into an eagerness to fault every aspect of technology from the slingshot to the space shuttle. This psychological climate affects perceptions and feeds an attitude that Edward Gottsman has called "cyberphobia" and others have termed "technophobia." In the market it manifests itself as resistance to, disregard for, and outright fear and dislike of technology. Marketing to cyberphobes successfully is important, for they are influential among online buyers and users and destructive of corporate and product images.

If the cyberphobe is ever going to become a user, a lot of internal change has to take place. Later in this chapter we will analyze in detail Westlaw's response to this issue in their brochure, *Discover the magic.* What they do is substitute one irrational idea for another on the logical marketing grounds that the likable and acceptable one they present, namely, magic, might unseat and displace the unfavorable one, cyberphobia. Substitution and displacement are shown to be one marketing approach to the problem. We will see CompuServe attack the same problem by making fun of science and letting the reader in on the joke—a "we-agree-with-you" approach to the problem. For marketing, this is a supreme challenge. Most of what is called "user friendly" in online systems is merely window dressing; the systems aren't idiot proof: in the main they are difficult to use. Marketing needs to work directly with product development to improve and simplify the products and services themselves. In this kind of project marketing should be acting as an "ombudsman" for both the cyberphobic and normal user, providing and advocating their respective points of view in an attempt to reduce to zero the grounds for criticism and reaction. When that is done, a way must be to found to tell the

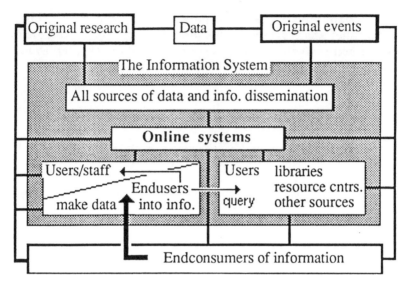

Figure 2.6. An information request from the endconsumer to the enduser.

story effectively to the most disaffected of cyberphobes and have the product and service bear out the promises made in its behalf.

According to high tech marketers like McKenna and Davidow, a company should be known for product satisfactions and benefits, and unconsciously recognized and warmly appreciated for its after-sale support. The satisfactions of the online user and enduser are important; they are key pathways for building the second sale. Post-sale support for both the user and the enduser is strongly indicated. It is accomplished by frequently stating and restating the traditional, emerging, and newly obtainable benefits of the service and its products so that need-gaps are minimized. Most of this has to occur long after formal instruction is over. Support should be both a consistent and persistent marketing effort. Advertising that trumpets the system, products, and benefits is one proven form of after-sale support, especially if a glamourous industry leader image can be presented.

2.6. Measures of Marketing Success

The extent to which the user, enduser, and sometimes even the end-consumer consider themselves well served by their direct online services is one of the new measures of marketing success. Another new criterion is the frequency of upward orders for information initiated by the endconsumer. (See figure 2.6.)

Along with all of the normal sales and marketing responsibilities, online marketing's concerns must be expanded to include ensuring that the databases are easily and cost-effectively searched and making sure where possible that the search artifacts are easily changed into information. The idea is to make sure that marketing is involved in helping the enduser and the endconsumer to become active consumers of online information. Marketing communication programs are charged with keeping the user and the enduser aware of the seller's system and stimulating the buyer's desire for repeated use (second sales) by making the benefits obvious and desirable.

Notes

1. E. Gottsman, "Note to Publishers: Electronic-Publishing Opportunities in Business and Professional Niche Markets," *New York: An Occasional Paper by the Edward J. Gottsman Company* 9 (1982):15.

3

INITIAL SALES

3.1. Introduction to Initial Sales in the Outline Industry

The initial sale can have one of two payoffs for the seller: when it results in a long-term contract being signed, the payoff is predictable income for the duration whether or not the system is used by the buyer; when the initial sale is merely the curtain raiser for the second sale (repeated use of the system by the buyer) the payoff is variable income each billing period, varying by the amount and style of the buyer's use. These two sales are quite different, and their marketing differences divide the initial buyers into two groups:

1. When the initial sale is made to a buyer who is neither the user nor the enduser of the service, these are most often contract sales: the buyer is mainly interested in the value of the service to the buying organization as a whole. Making this sale requires cogent arguments stressing benefits to the buying organization and may have little to do with the actual operations of the system.
2. When the initial sale is made to a buyer who is both the decision maker and the user, one who both buys the service and uses a keyboard, this sale must include a limited and effective demonstration of the actual operations of the system.

Marketing managers and sales experts are adamant that no prospective buyer should be allowed to get bogged down in either the operational details of the service or the intricacies of pricing, or the sale can be lost. Nor should marketing programs in support of either of these sales get mired in these issues. The initial sale situation as a whole is shown in figure 3.1, with both branches of the tree demanding different marketing and sales tactics.

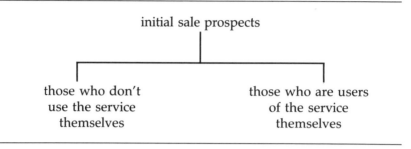

initial sale prospects

those who don't
use the service
themselves

those who are users
of the service
themselves

Figure 3.1. Two types of initial sales prospects.

As shown in figure 3.1, there are two kinds of initial buyers: those who rarely see the system after it is installed (remote buyers); and those who use it themselves (hands-on buyers). The differences are vividly demographic: remote buyers are often the CEO's, CFO's, or MIS managers, organizational executives, senior staff, and decision makers; hands-on buyers are often working librarians, research assistants, or individual knowledge workers. Figure 3.2 shows the situation.

Figure 3.2 also shows that the marketer has a second sale opportunity to use the individual influences working on both types of

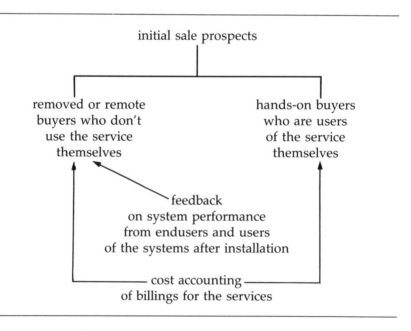

initial sale prospects

removed or remote
buyers who don't
use the service
themselves

hands-on buyers
who are users
of the service
themselves

feedback
on system performance
from endusers and users
of the systems after installation

cost accounting
of billings for the services

Figure 3.2. Initial sales prospects, by type of feedback.

initial buyers. The seller can positively manage the impression that billing and service-related marketing communications make on the initial buyer. The opportunity arises because that is one of the few remaining points of contact after the initial sale is made. Particularly important is running a program designed to influence the quality of the feedback that the remote buyer gets from his designated users and other endusers. One of the best ways to do this is by having marketing deeply involved in client communications, billing, product development, user instruction, and service-feature communications.

3.2. The Initial Buyer's Unique Concerns Are Relevant to Marketing Planning

Marketing uses the concerns of initial buyers as tactical stepping stones in marketing programs. They provide a solid context for pointed appeals in selling. Concerns may range over the following commonly encountered issues:

For Both Types of Initial Buyers

- A time deadline on purchase decisions is always there and is always significant in the sale. It must be identified and accommodated in the marketing and sales processes.
- The decision to subscribe to an online service carries enough financial risk (partly because of the pricing muddle) to prompt formal risk assessment in some situations. Helping the removed initial sales buyer in a positive risk/regret analysis should be one of the strongest efforts in initial sales marketing.
- If a buyer is already committed to an installed online system, he is evaluating the risks and costs (in both time and dollars) of switching to or adding a new one. The seller must be able to accurately calculate the total cost/benefit of switching and system use. The seller must realistically accept that his best possible outline may be a percent share of the buyer's total business.
- Both types of buyers are often proactive in information gathering on specific online industry products and pricing. Their knowledge can be used to shorten the marketing and sales process when the buyer's level of understanding can be identified and understood. The seller must know the competition inside and out, especially their pricing.
- In some cases, both types of buyers may well have a detailed overview of the information market, the whole range of competing online services, database products, and pricing based on their experience and training. The seller must let the buyer

tell him what he knows in these instances, and marketing communications must be sensitive to the knowledge of these well-informed buyers.

- Both types of buyers are accustomed to making system-wide choices and buying decisions, even if they are limited to their own systems and small organizations. The seller shouldn't be afraid to ask for the business at the appropriate time after determining that the person he is seeing is the final decision maker and buyer.

For Remote Initial Buyers

- The principal benefit of the service may be seen as a new capability for getting data and therefore improved reporting and decision making within the management tier of the buying organization. Not all industry analysts agree that online services both lower the cost and improve the effectiveness of the executive echelon of an organization, but computer and online service buying patterns indicate that many initial sales prospects believe it.
- Remote buyers often look at the overall information needs of their entire organization (even if they are confined in scope to just one person's needs and a small organization). Overall benefits must be analyzed, understood, and communicated in the frame of reference of this type of buyer's organizational needs.

For Hands-On Initial Buyers

Hands-on initial buyers want the same overall benefits as other initial buyers but with the added attractions of (1) gaining the personal pleasure of using electronic and automated communications and research tools, (2) getting increased social rewards for doing better work, and (3) gaining the increased sense of personal worth fostered by new levels of productivity obtained through enriched information management and use of the system. These personal accomplishments should be anticipated by marketing communications.

3.3. Other Marketing Issues in the Initial Sale

POSITIONING

Keeping the product's name and benefits in front of the initial sale prospect is one of the overriding tasks of marketing. How that is done and what it accomplishes in the mind of the prospect (and user) is called *positioning*. The central communication issue is memorably influencing the customer's awareness of, use, and involvement with the service and its benefits by creating an indelible impression of the benefits of use. The task is one of ideas and images. In communications a clear distinction must be observed between the first and second sales: the first is more removed and rational in character than the second because of the buying aim, and marketing communications must be suitably rational; the second is closer in and more emotional because the service will become, or is now, a dynamic part of the user's life, and, therefore, is a personal matter. Marketing communication tactics can focus on these facts and exploit them in developing a unique position for the product in the mind of the user.

THE "HIGH TECH" FACTOR

Online services are, for good or ill, part of the world of telecommunications and computers. Initial buyers see themselves as subject to the complex social and marketing forces of the high tech market. "The over enthusiastic vendors and other boosters of automation and the computer age are hoist on their own petards," writes Lynn M. Salerno in the *Harvard Business Review.* "In trying to sell computers, literally and figuratively, they have made the task of mastering them look too easy and the attainable rewards appear too great. Now buyers are wary, and many products remain on the shelf. Perhaps it has become clear that the public has some idea of what it needs and wants, even when dazzling electronics are involved."[1] As a consequence, marketing to a buyer in the high tech arena requires awareness of a built-in twofold handicap: cynicism and distrust are extended to company claims and products; and the penalties of adoption (e.g., getting the unproven system, or paying too much for too little technology) are seen as traps. This is a gap between expectations that marketing can bridge. In many cases in high tech sales the gap is painfully real on both sides—the numbers of unused, outmoded, and unusable computers gathering dust in homes and offices throughout the United States and Great Britain is the classic example. Online services have gaps in the buyer's perception and use of their products and services too, but to a lesser degree than some other types of high tech products and services.

FLAT-RATE PRICING

No seller using variable or mixed pricing schemes has rationalized his pricing, nor is he able to explain his pricing easily to the buyer.

The buyer flies blind on total price in any billing period or budget cycle, a serious risk-management disadvantage for him in the era of spread-sheet budgeting, spread-sheet management and spread-sheet thinking. Buyers hunger for some level of predictability in pricing given the risk-management pressures from the accounting department. Often it is expressed as a wistful desire for flat-rate (so much per hour) pricing. Paradoxically, flat-rate pricing, so "ideally advantageous" in the mind of buyer, is a disincentive to the seller to strive for the most efficient use of his major capital investment, the mainframe computer.

3.4. Marketing Communications in Initial Sales

Few online organizations have sales forces. Since most depend on visual communications and telemarketing for making their sales, visual communication is of special interest to online marketers. Our discussion will be confined to the print medium. Most marketing projects use both words and pictures to get the message across to the buyer. Given these opportunities and responsibilities online marketers must know how to estimate the content and effectiveness of the words and pictures in their communication materials. The examples in this book will allow the reader to consider how visual communications work for the online industry.

Three print ads are included in this chapter as examples of current advertising practice in support of the initial sale in the online industry. Each selection is emblematic of one of the three main styles of presentation in use in the industry: (1) fantasy, (2) quasi-documentary, and (3) documentary. The examples also show the general range of what has been attempted in advertising over the last few years. A detailed analysis of the meanings found in the advertisement's copy and imagery is contrasted and compared with those of other advertisements. The marketing themes are shown by either their absence or their presence in the comparisons.

All of the examples in this chapter are presumed on their internal and external evidence to be aimed at the initial buyer. Advertisements for the initial sale contain copy and art structured to achieve that specific sale. In theory, copy and art should stress the added values of the products and services, show the benefits to buying organizations and, to a much lesser degree, point out the benefits to the hands-on users of the system.

A simple approach to advertising was once summarized by a print salesman who liked to say, "Don't overthink your advertising and marketing; just tell the story, make it look good and get it to the right audience." His reductionist approach may be right for a well-known tangible product in a mature industry, but even that application is highly doubtful. In the immature online industry, his kind of reduction will only make matters worse. The interlocked and complex service-and-use benefits are too difficult to position, visualize, and describe dramatically and persuasively to permit it.

Print advertising and printed marketing communications have built the online industry. Print is the communication medium of the online industry because its superior capacity for data permits lengthy and complicated sales stories like those of the online industry to be told well. Its expandability into presentations of considerable length (some new product introductions in high tech run to twenty-four pages per section) coupled with affordable frequency-of-appearance rates makes print the cost-effective medium for complex product messages, and consequently for most high-tech advertising. Television is the fashionable advertising medium in the United States but few online firms can afford to experiment with it. The results are not yet in from the few that have.

In one sense marketers can be thought of as being in the representation business. To understand this concept one must grasp the basic principal of representation, namely: when we are trying to tell or show someone something we often choose to create a representation of the "something" in words, pictures, gestures, etc., in the hope that the audience will understand our representation and communication will be successful. When used in this sense, representation means "to offer again, in a different form, that which exists in real life or in our imagination." In marketing, "offerings" are usually in two symbolic formats: words (linguistic representations) and pictures (artistic representations). Both words and pictures are components of signs. The analysis of signs and symbols in advertising and marketing communications is called psychological semiotics, iconology, semiotics, or image decoding depending on one's preference and training. The object of this kind of analysis is "to help . . . understand the many messages . . . advertising is transmitting to consumers on both a conscious and subconscious level. Ads have always been rich with psychological imagery, but advertisers now are trying harder to control and manipulate the symbols."[2]

Word and picture schemes can be reduced to their basic parts for analysis. Any representation can be defined by three variables that, for our purposes, can be called: (1) explicit copy, (2) implicit copy, and (3) audience. The variables have fairly precise categorical limits that can be identified in context and then judged on their merit. While this approach takes a few moments to apply and a few tries to learn, it overcomes the major problem of dealing with the whole communication all at once, which can be both misleading and confusing. Analysis by variable works to improve creative quality and content because representations are composed of the external results of the creative process. Variables can be mapped and understood in either a proposed or an existing communication scheme, agreed to on their merits, disputed on their public evidence, and compared and contrasted with the same variables as they are used in other marketing communications for similar products or services for the same or similar audiences. From these discussions and analyses much can be done to specifically improve the quality and content of advertising and marketing communications.

The variables are defined here as:[3]

Explicit Copy. "The Content As Represented." The reality, ideas, and experiences that we use words and pictures to describe and depict in marketing communications.

Implicit Copy. "Making Representation Concrete." The meanings that arise from the combinations of images, words, shapes, sizes, physical arrangement, styles, colors, and other physical, technical, and media details of marketing communications.

Audiences. "The human contingent." Those who produce the marketing communications, who are in the target market of the communication's producers, and all who may comprehend or be influenced by the communications including the competition.

Visual and semiotic research in marketing communications and extensive experience with copy and images in high tech has taught me that the three variables are actively interdependent in a specific communication context; in practice a change in one variable (e.g., replacing the picture in an advertisement but not rewriting the copy) almost always leads to further creative work on the copy to rebalance and refocus the whole after the new picture has been inserted. Examining the pattern of interaction among the variables is a check of the alignment with marketing objectives. There are over fifty examples of this method in this book. The reader will soon become familiar with it if he or she will read the examples carefully and reconsider the definitions of the variables provided at the start of each section where analysis is applied. Here is the first example.

EXPLICIT COPY CompuServe calls the advertisement shown in plate 3.3 their basic "primer," but it is anything but scholastic. It is a fantasy advertisement that weaves and dodges with the speed and agility of a bantamweight boxer. Several layers of meaning are rapidly shuffled around to keep reader interest high (e.g., the secondary theme is the most visually prominent; great inventions of the past were breakthrough inventions all right, but essentially simple ones that were difficult to exploit and apply—so simple, in fact, they are almost laughable). The great inventions of today, namely, computers and information services, are much more complicated to grasp, use, and absorb, but the payoff is immediate and gratifying. The primary theme (an appeal aimed at the home PC owner) is introduced later in the copy and, significantly for the overall meaning of the advertisement, in the context established by the secondary theme. The argument is that one's home PC is gathering dust because it's too hard to understand, like, and use, and here, at last, is a sophisticated computer-based invention that adds real productivity without adding any baffling complications because anyone can use it. It plays directly to cyberphobia and antihigh tech feelings by first recognizing them frankly and second offering an antidote to frustration and defeat.

The secondary theme, "Breakthrough," is a feint used to keep the reader's attention and to keep the context light. A cleverly entitled list of the features of the service is presented in well chosen and memorable lay terms with highlighted benefits. The optimistic intent of all this is the conversion of static cyberphobia into active hope and then into use. The active change agent offered to the buyer is the promise of new benefits obtained with the user's present low level of systems mastery. A further inducement is price. The price/value appeal argues that with just a little more investment the PC can be made to pay off—a solid benefit. The tone of the presentation is playful throughout this fantasy presentation. The text is breezy and so are the pictures. Eight small photos and cartoons depict fanciful situations. A coupon is provided.

IMPLICIT COPY   Attention has been paid to the use of expressive typefaces with high contrast to each other. The type has been organized into small copy units suitable for a reader with a short attention span. Text is the dominant presentation of this advertisement. It is designed to be read in small gulps. The advertisement is presented in magazine format on two pages in four colors. The overall visual look of the advertisement is inviting and open.

AUDIENCES   The marketing plan is to approach the initial buyer as a buffaloed user/enduser. The advertisement is a frank discussion of disappointment. It reflects the mind set and respects it, indeed, it capitalizes on it. This advertisement recognizes the negative effects of the high tech environment as important to the reader. The product is positioned as a "cure" of sorts. Ridicule of science and technology is one of the major themes of the advertisement designed to bring the reader to the side of the seller. The final appeal, "CompuServe makes the most of any computer," is probably read by the audience as "CompuServe makes the most of any computer user."

SOME HISTORIC BREAKTHROUGH
DON'T TAKE AS MUCH EXPLAININ
AS COMPUSERVE.

But then, some historic breakthroughs could only take you from the cave to the tar pits and back again.

CompuServe, on the other hand, makes a considerably more civilized contribution to your life.

It turns that marvel of the 20th century, the personal computer, into something useful.

Unlike most personal computer products you read about, CompuServe is an information service. It isn't software. It isn't hardware. And you don't even have to know a thing about programming to use it. You subscribe to CompuServe —and 24 hours a day, 7 days a week, it puts a universe of information, entertainment and communications right at your fingertips.

A few of the hundreds of things you can do with CompuServe.

COMMUNICATE

EasyPlex™ Electronic Mail lets even beginners compose, edit, send and file messages the first time they get online. It puts friends, relatives and

business associates—anywhere in the country — in constant, convenient touch.

CB Simulator features 72 channels for "talking" with thousands of other enthusiastic subscribers throughout the country and Canada. The chatter is frequently hilarious, the "handles" unforgettable, and the friendships hard and fast.

More than 100 Forums welcome your participation in "discussions" on all sorts of topics. There are Forums for computer owners, gourmet cooks, veterinarians, pilots, golfers, musicians, you name it! Also, Electronic Conferencing lets businesses put heads together without anyone having to leave the shop.

Bulletin Boards let you "post" messages where thousands will see them. You can use our National Bulletin Board or the specialized Bulletin Boards found in just about every Forum.

HAVE FUN

Our full range of games includes "You Guessed It!", the first online TV-style game show you play for real prizes; and MegaWars III, offering the

ultimate in interactive excitement. And there are board, parlor, sport and educational games to play alo or against other subscribers throughout the country.

Movie Reviews keep that big night at the movies from being five star mistake.

SHOP

THE ELECTRONIC MALL™ give you convenient, 24-hour-a-day, 7-day-a-week shopping for name brand goods and services at disco prices from nationally known stor and businesses.

SAVE ON TRIPS

Travelshopper℠ lets you scan flight availabilities (on virtually any airline — world-wide), find airfare bargains and orde tickets right on your computer.

Worldwide Exchange sets you u with the perfect yacht, condo, villa or whatever it takes to make your n vacation *a vacation*.

A to Z Travel/News Service provides the latest travel news plus complete information on over 20,0 hotels worldwide.

Figure 3.3. An advertisement by CompuServe. *Courtesy of CompuServe Incorporated.*

MAKE PHI BETA KAPPA

Grolier's Academic American Encyclopedia's Electronic Edition delivers a complete set of encyclopedias right to your living room just in time for today's homework. It's continuously updated... and doesn't take an inch of extra shelf space.

The College Board, operated by the College Entrance Examination Board, gives tips on preparing for the SAT, choosing a college and getting financial aid.

KEEP HEALTHY

Healthnet will never replace a real, live doctor—but it is an excellent and readily available source of health and medical information for the public.

Human Sexuality gives the civilization that put a man on the moon an intelligent alternative to the daily "Advice to the Lovelorn" columns. Hundreds turn to it for real answers.

BE INFORMED

All the latest news is at your fingertips. Sources include the AP news wire (covering all 50 states plus national news), the Washington Post, USA TODAY Update, specialized business and trade publications and more. You can find out instantly what Congress did yesterday; who finally won the game; and what's happening back in Oskaloosa with the touch of a button. And our electronic clipping service lets you tell us what to watch for. We'll electronically find, clip and file news for you...to read whenever you'd like.

INVEST WISELY

Comprehensive investment help just might tell you more about the stock you're looking at than the company's Chairman of the Board knows. (Don't know who he is? Chances are, we can fill you in on that, too.) CompuServe gives you complete statistics on over 10,000 NYSE, AMEX and OTC securities. Historic trading statistics on over 50,000

stocks, bonds, funds, issues and options. Five years of daily commodity quotes. Standard & Poor's. Value Line. And more than a dozen other investment tools.

Site II facilitates business decisions by providing you with demographic and sales potential information by state, county and zip code for the entire country.

National and Canadian business wires provide continuously updated news and press releases on hundreds of companies worldwide.

GET SPECIALIZED INFORMATION

Pilots get personalized flight plans, weather briefings, weather and radar maps, newsletters, etc.

Entrepreneurs use CompuServe too for complete step-by-step guidelines on how to incorporate the IBMs of tomorrow.

Lawyers, doctors, engineers, military veterans and businessmen of all types use similar specialized CompuServe resources pertinent to their unique needs.

And now for the pleasant surprise.

Although CompuServe makes the most of any computer, it's a remarkable value. With CompuServe, you get low start-up costs, low usage charges and local phone-call access in most major metropolitan areas.

Here's exactly how to use CompuServe.

First, relax.

There are no advanced computer skills required.

In fact, if you know how to buy breakfast, you already have the know-how you'll need to access any subject in our system. That's because it's "menu-driven," so beginners can simply read the menus (lists of options) that appear on their screens and then type in their selections.

Experts can skip the menus and just type in "GO" followed by the abbreviation for whatever topic they're after.

In case you ever get lost or confused, just type in "H" for help, and we'll immediately cut in with instructions that should save the day.

Besides, you can either ask questions online through our Feedback service or phone our Customer Service Department.

How to subscribe.

To access CompuServe, you'll need a CompuServe Subscription Kit, a computer, a modem to connect your computer to your phone, and in some cases, easy-to-use communications software. (Check the information that comes with your modem.)

With your Subscription Kit, you'll receive:

■ a $25 usage credit.
■ a complete hardcover Users Guide.
■ your own exclusive user ID number and preliminary password.
■ a subscription to CompuServe's monthly magazine, *Online Today.*

Call **800-848-8199** (in Ohio, 614-457-0802) to order your Subscription Kit or to receive more information. Or mail this coupon.

Kits are also available in computer stores, electronic equipment outlets and household catalogs. You can also subscribe with materials you'll find packed right in with many computers and modems sold today.

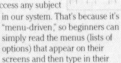

After several years of widespread use this advertisement was updated into the version shown in figure 3.4. The revisions show that the idea of the primer advertisement remains important in the American market. The coupon has been eliminated as unproductive of qualified leads, but the 800 number has been retained. The revised advertisement is simpler in appearance and copy structure but the central themes are retained.

EXPLICIT COPY   This is a quasi-documentary advertisement for Mead Data Central. Mead provides "global" information access on its Lexis/Nexis services. There are two allied ideas at work here: Lexis/Nexis is advanced beyond the state of the art of the rest of the online industry (a major claim), and the AT&T PC is the best terminal from which to access the "world" (another major claim). This is a tandem argument of two "bests." Each brand lends its credibility and glamour to the other. The reality evoked by this exchange is that these two systems smoothly complement and reinforce each other; they fuse into a single powerful information and computing system.

The marketing plan is to reach the AT&T PC buyer as a pre-qualified initial buyer for the Mead system. The high front-end pricing of the service argues for this kind of approach. The buyer is shown at the bottom of the advertisement. His attitude is one of relaxed satisfaction with his search results. Since he is shown standing by a terminal, not using one, he is read as a removed initial buyer. He conveys the sense of an enduser. The reader is encouraged to become like him by having both the AT&T PC and the Mead service.

IMPLICIT COPY.   The advertisement was printed in black and white in magazine format. The typefaces express a conservative up-to-dateness. The text is brief and concise. The image at the top of the page is dominant and is the context for interpretation of the copy and for all meanings. The advertisement urges the reader to appreciate the added values of the association of the two brands and surrounds the message with a strong appeal to competitive edge through high technology and database use. Power leads to success, mastery, and survival. These are the tools of power.

AUDIENCES   The targeted audiences are the AT&T PC buyer; those glamoured by the AT&T PC; other buyers of top-of-the-line computers, Lexis/Nexis subscribers seeking to upgrade their computer systems; and those impressed by Mead's services. (There may be some confusion in the audiences addressed in this advertisement by the attempt to reach both the removed and the hands-on buyer with the same message.)

The PHINet Campaign

For years Prentice Hall has published a federal taxes looseleaf service, *P-H Federal Taxes*, and several years ago it introduced its electronic database version, PHINet. In the introductory advertisement of the PHINet campaign (not shown here), the message content and actual physical surface area were divided roughly 2/3 for online and 1/3 for books. This degree of imbalance failed to push PHINet into a position of dominance. The weighting could be read as a defensive move to protect the positioning and sales of the book product, and not as a sales pitch for the online product.

The documentary format and style of the original advertisement didn't allow room for any evocative expression of the added values of PHINet, like those we have seen in the CompuServe and Mead Data Central advertisements. The result was ambiguity about the PHINet product. The positioning of PHINet could alternatively be read as a cosmetic attempt merely to lend up-to-dateness to the looseleaf system. This presentation raised doubts about PHINet's worth. The doubt was reinforced by the obvious absence of a burning desire on the part of Prentice Hall to switch the buyer from books to PHINet. There was no "sell" for either product in the original advertisement. A coupon included in the original advertisement was too small to be practical and no 800 number was given.

Unlike the other advertisements we've seen where the desire to sell online services was foremost, Prentice Hall's choices suggest that it could not make a strong exclusive pitch for PHINet. The drawbacks of this approach demonstrate the virtues of a strong single-minded desire for sales, a dynamic imbalance in marketing presentations. These devices get the message out. They dramatize the product, and boldly ask for the business. Their absence is a powerful message too, as seen in both the first and second PHINet advertisements.

The second advertisement, figure 3.6, attempted to resolve favorably some of the issues in the PHINet campaign. It tried to build on the original theme—"the switch is on"—by honoring the content and the documentary format of the first advertisement. It introduced the whimsy of literally plugging the terminal into the books, a more imaginative device for keeping the authority and creditability balance between the book system and the online system visible and intact. This occurs (again), however, at the expense of a strong all-out sell for the PHINet system, in spite of the introduction of a new logo, and heavier emphasis on the features of the PHINet system in the copy. In this version, the coupon has been eliminated and no 800 number is given.

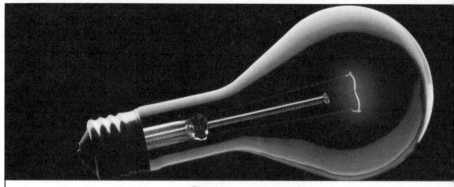

COMPUSERVE.
YOU DON'T HAVE TO KNOW HOW IT WORK
TO APPRECIATE ALL IT CAN DO.

You don't have to know about hardware. You don't have to know about software. All you have to know is that CompuServe is a computer information service. You subscribe to it. And in return, you have access to an incredible amount of information, entertainment, communications and services right at your fingertips.

Here are a few of the hundreds of things you can do with CompuServe.

COMMUNICATE

Even beginners can compose, edit, send and file messages the first time they go online with CompuServe's **EasyPlex™ Electronic Mail.** Friends, relatives and business associates— anywhere in the country—can stay in constant, convenient touch.

CB Simulator features 72 channels for "talking" with thousands of other subscribers throughout the country and Canada. The chatter is frequently hilarious, the "handles" unforgettable and the friendships hard and fast.

More than 100 CompuServe Forums welcome your participation in discussions on all sorts of topics. There are Forums for gourmet cooks, golfers, musicians, pilots, sailors and more, all designed to show you how easy and fun it can be to get the most out of your computer.

If you want to learn more about your computer system, CompuServe's at your service. Our **Users Forums** cater to specific computer makes and models, and offer information and expertise on many different types of machines. You'll find electronic editions of popular computer periodicals. You can even find free software.

And if you need answers to software questions, seek out a **Software Forum.** You can often find solutions quickly and easily online.

Bulletin Boards let you post messages where thousands will see them. Use our National Bulletin Board or the specialized bulletin boards found in almost every Forum.

HAVE FUN

You'll find all sorts of sports and entertainment trivia games, plus brain-teasing educational games. You can go it alone or compete against players from all over the country. Test your wits in the only online TV-style game show with real prizes. Then, when you're ready, go for the ultimate in excitement and get into one of our interactive space adventures.

CompuServe's **movie reviews** kee that big night at the movies from being a five-star mistake. **Soap opera updates** keep you up on all the latest turmoils and tragedies on your favorite daytime dramas.

For leisure-time reading and relaxing, look into the electronic editions of some of your favorite magazines, including OMNI On-Line.

SHOP

CompuServe's **ELECTRONIC MAL** lets you take a coast-to-coast shopping spree without ever leaving home. It's a exciting and easy way to shop online, buying name-brand goods and service from nationally known merchants.

SAVE ON TRIPS

CompuServe's travel services let you control your own travel arrangements through the convenience of your personal computer. Scan flight availabilities on almost any airline worldwide. Find airfare bargains, then book your own flight online.

Figure 3.4. Revised version of the CompuServe advertisement. *Courtesy of CompuServe Incorporated.*

Figure 3.5. An advertisement by Mead Data Central. © *Mead Data Central, Inc.*

Figure 3.6. An advertisement by Prentice Hall. *Advertising art courtesy of PHINet,®️ The Prentice Hall Information Network* (Simon and Schuster Professional Information Group).

EXPLICIT COPY "Prepare at Your Own Risk" is the newest advertisement in the campaign and it cuts new ground. For the first time a major benefit dominates, namely, enhanced risk management through PHINet's electronic mastery of the tax information environment. The emergence of this theme automatically brings the user of the system into the spotlight. Copy arguments such as, "due diligence doesn't have to mean 300 hours spent plowing through 3000 zillion cases" state the efficiency advantage of PHINet over manual or paper systems in user terms. There is no coupon or 800 number in this version.

IMPLICIT COPY Up to this point in the campaign, the advertisements have been very documentary, undramatic, and "grayed." Typefaces have been conservative and muted. Figure 3.7 has boldness, graphic impact and up-to-date styling throughout. The copy is brisk and to the point. It breaks with the stylistic history of the campaign.

AUDIENCES All of the ads in the campaign have been directed at initial buyers; the latest "Prepared at Your Own Risk" (figure 3.7) is specifically for the hands-on buyer. The model of the buyer remains that of a hands-on user of the looseleaf book who is either cyberphobic, wedded to books (not the same thing), or both. This hesitation arises because the average PHINet user, the tax attorney or accountant, is not generally rated as aggressive, changeable, or progressive, a market characteristic so well understood that it has even been the subject of comment in the *Wall Street Journal*. In the first two ads, this model of the audience, when used by a publisher who thought "books," and who believed that the initial buyer might not accept online systems, produced a very conservative result. In the current advertisement the user is treated as if he or she is progressive and is even recognized as an inherent risk taker. The copy and art of the advertisement reflect the changes in the audience model.

CONCLUSIONS From comparative analysis of these advertisements an estimate of the marketing strategies for initial sales in the online industry can be made. The advertisements reveal the marketing styles of the firms, their reading of the market, their estimate of the competitive factors, their awareness of the high-tech environment, and their unique conceptions of the added values of their services.

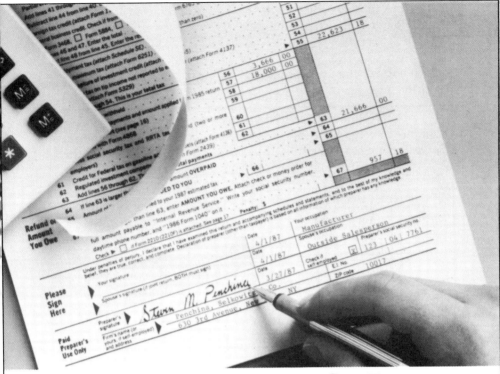

PREPARE AT YOUR OWN RISK.

It's not going to be business as usual anymore.

Because now, preparing taxes is likely to be as big a legal responsibility as paying them. And a lot more work.

But if you can't do anything about the proposed IRS regulations calling for "substantial authority," you can at least make them a lot easier to live with.

Announcing PHINet™ (pronounced FI · net) from Prentice Hall: the first complete on-line tax research and information service available.

© 1987 Prentice Hall Information Services

With PHINet, "due diligence" doesn't have to mean 300 hours spent plowing through 3 zillion cases. In fact, you don't work serially case by case at all. Because unlike competitive tax research services, PHINet's unique research system lets you locate the case you want and fully ascertain its authority in a matter of minutes.

And by citing additional authority, PHINet even makes weighing both sides of the issue easier (something else other tax information services fail to do).

Finally, PHINet is the only on-

line tax research and information service that's adaptable to whatever computer system your company has—and PHINet is ready to use right now.

We can't promise that you won't have any sleepless nights because of the proposed IRS regulations. But with PHINet, you'll be able to rest a whole lot easier.

For more information, call collect (212) 373-8217 or write to: PHINet, 1 Gulf + Western Plaza, 18th Floor, New York, NY 10023.

PRENTICE HALL
INFORMATION SERVICES

Figure 3.7. An advertisement by Prentice Hall. *Advertising art courtesy of PHINet,®* The Prentice Hall Information Network (Simon and Schuster Professional Information Group).

Note that advertisements are highly flexible in the range of explicit content they communicate.

Explicit copy of the advertisements

Type	Ideas	Reality	Experience
Compu-Serve	Technology isn't such a big deal unless you can use it	High tech is something the buyer must overcome	Get new use out of a poor investment in the home PC
Mead	AT&T technology and Mead online technology are both leaders	High tech is no barrier to this initial buyer	Only the very best systems will give the user an edge
Prentice Hall	Risk management in tax work can be enhanced by automation	High tech may or may not be acceptable to the buyer	Coping with change will be easier and safer

The shape and form systems of advertisements allow for a wide range of implicit copy expressions used either to reinforce or to play down important aspects of the messages.

Implicit copy of the advertisements

Type	Forms	Letters	Colors
Compu-Serve	Copy dominant, with headlines and images secondary	Informal and modern	4 color
Mead	Visually dominant imagery, copy secondary	Formal and modern	Black and white
Prentice Hall	Visually dominant headline, imagery and copy secondary	Modern, uptempo	Black and white

All of the people who create, make and read advertisements are numbered among their influential audiences.

Audiences

Type	Producers	Perceivers	Society
Compu-Serve	Marketing	Hand-on initial buyers who are PC owners un-happy with the productivity of their invest-ments	The home user
Mead	Marketing	Remote initial buyers who may also be buyers of the AT&T systems	Business and government
Prentice Hall	Marketing	Hands-on initial buyers who may also be users of P.H.'s manuals	Accounting professionals

Figure 3.8. Comparison of the use of three communication variables in the CompuServe, Mead, and Prentice Hall advertisements.

3.5. Types Of Visual Communications in Initial Sales

Advertising has the advantage of special clarity—a singleness of purpose in a highly controlled context. Other marketing materials designed to support sales and persuade the buyer suffer from all of the conflicts inherent in sales. At the expense of singleness of purpose, multiple communication missions are predicted for and built in to most online sales and marketing brochures as an economy measure. As a result a hybrid approach has developed that I call the *omnibus brochure* (OB). The typical mission range for OB's include the trade show, the sales call, direct mail, or all of the above. To understand this brochure one must examine the missions imposed on it.

THE SALES CALL SUPPORT MISSION

The personal sales call is expensive. The average sales call in the United States costs the seller over $250 per unit. Because of cost, calls are made on well-qualified prospects or potential buyers (those who may have been softened up in advance by direct mail or telemarketing). The OB used in the sales call is, ideally, reviewed line-by-line with the prospective buyer and then left behind as a reference and reselling aid. There is no direct competition during the actual sales call from other competing literature (even though it may be present in the room or stored in the files of the buyer). The OB is supplemented by the oral and visual sales pitches of the sales representative. The OB is probably read again by the potential buyer after the sales call is over. It is often accompanied by other sales-specific materials reinforcing the message and enhancing the reader's understanding. Its mission is to supplement the sales call itself and to be a calling card and silent spokesperson for the online service after the call is ended. It must be attractive, comprehensive, persuasive, and a buyer-centered selling aid.

TRADE SHOW SUPPORT MISSION

A trade show is a mid-priced sales call on those who stop at the table or booth. Trade show attendance can cost an online organization as much as $25-50,000 on each occasion. The cost is offset by the volume of traffic at the show, which lowers the cost of talking to a self-qualified potential buyer well beneath that of a personal sales call (total exhibit cost ÷ total booth traffic = cost of sales call). Even though the trade show attendee is a self-qualified and self-selected audience who is interested in the topic of the trade show, the audience is composed of hard-to-sort-out groups of "lookers" and "potential buyers." (Many devices are used to separate these two groups at shows.) The spirited tempo of shows usually means that any literature given out is examined in detail later, and gathering literature at trade shows is a minor curatorial hobby for some attendees. In this sales environment the seller's literature is competing with all of the other sales literature in circulation at the show just as much as the booths compete for the viewer's attention. Visual impact counts. The OB is supplemented at a show with the visual contents of the booth and any oral messages and demonstrations given by the sales staff. An OB may be given to the buyer singly or, better yet, with supplementary materials in an omnibus information kit and, best of all, as part of a memorable demonstration of the online system. Naturally, there is no personalized cover letter on the brochure directed to the buyer's specific interests, so some degree of sales focus is sacrificed.

DIRECT MAIL MISSION

This is the cheapest sales call of all. In the late 1980's, most personalized mailings can be made to the domestic potential buyer for under $20 per unit. The OB may be read by the prospect or his designee, at his discretion. It is in direct competition with other sales literature from all sources; to succeed it has to win the Battle of the In Basket. In this sense it must stand alone, a visually aggressive and complete sales call. To do so effectively it must have a technology for prequalifying the prospect or closing the sale bound or inserted into the book or associated to it physically (usually the technology is a return postage-paid envelope and/or card, or a United States 800 telephone number to be called toll free). The OB always arrives with a cover letter addressed to the buyer by his name and title that focuses the argument of the brochure down to a specific appeal to the needs of the buyer (if they are known or knowable). It has a primary standalone sales mission and must function accordingly, even if it is supported by telemarketing activities. The envelope in which the OB is sent is critical to the success of the mailing. It must encourage the buyer to open the package by promising a benefit for doing so. The omnibus brochure, above all else, must be worth the effort of opening the envelope and worth keeping, once it has been read. A lot of direct mail misses the mark because of complications in the selection of mailing lists and in mismatching the wide scope of the OB with the narrow interests of the prospect.

3.6. Three Types of Omnibus Brochures are in Use in the Industry

Three general formats have evolved: fantasy, quasi-documentary, and documentary. Each format fills a tactical marketing and sales niche that is discussed below, along with a representative visual example taken from each type of brochure.

EXPLICIT COPY   This is an example of a fantasy brochure. The theme is "Superiority Is no Illusion" and the content is designed as a specific counter sell to Mead's Lexis Service, which is referred to

Discover the magic.

Figure 3.9.   Cover of the Westlaw brochure. © 1985. *Reprinted with permission by West Publishing Co., St. Paul, Minn.*

by name. The magic metaphor is so complex that I will confine my analysis to the central idea, which is that the magician, shown on the front cover of the brochure, transforms himself into a working lawyer by the end of the brochure. Westlaw "magic" is incorporated directly into the lawyer. Magic seems to evade a direct confrontation with the reality of Lexis. If all that one had to offer was magic there would be a major product development and positioning problem. The credibility issue raised by the magic claim is offset by placing next in sequence to each claim for magic a documentary claim for the system. The claim is composed of factual text and images asserting the exact nature of Westlaw's position.

In summary, the communication and editorial plan is that magic stands for benefits, and fact tells the features of the system. Magic, then, refers to all of the added values of the brand. This tactic hopefully overcomes the buyer's current awareness or use of Lexis, or his reservations about the use of new or unfamiliar research technologies by the substitution of a more palatable, or, in this case, whimsical idea. The magical events visualized throughout the brochure symbolize ease of use and seamless interaction among the user, the online system, and Westlaw's printed reference systems. This theme addresses the complex and threatening problems of office automation, reference management, and user cyberphobia by substitution—it says, substitute our notion of "magic" (wink) for these feelings and you don't have to deal with them as technical realities. Also it says, you already know how to use our books (West Publishing is a major publisher of legal texts), therefore you already know most of what you need to know to use our online system; in fact, used together, it's just magic, and so effortless you look like a magician to your clients and staff.

IMPLICIT COPY   Fantasy illustrations are contrasted with factual photographs throughout the six spreads of the brochure. Production values are quite high—four-color printing, slick paper, a large format, matching envelope, etc. The brochure is high quality, memorable, attention getting, and valuable enough to keep.

AUDIENCES   Fantasy, when used as a thematic appeal in a major brochure, suggests that, in Westlaw's opinion, prospective remote and hands-on buyers might like to consider their practice of law as magical, powerful, or effortless, and that Westlaw's systems can provide that fantasy fulfillment.

EXPLICIT COPY   British Telecom's brochure is an example of the quasi-documentary brochure. It positions the City Business System (CBS) as the latest communication technology serving the rapidly expanding global financial services market. The appeal developed in the brochure is that CBS is an advanced system for use now and in the forseeable technical future. The overall theme, understated on the cover, is that multiple levels of data and information can be obtained instantly and accurately through a single touch-controlled system that is also used to place calls and orders instantly in markets anywhere.

The world is shown as reachable over the system, a benefit to the dealer. The event is dramatized several times in the brochure, with the whole presentation creating a useful interpretative context

Figure 3.10. An internal spread from the Westlaw brochure. ©1985 *Reprinted with permission by West Publishing Co., St. Paul, Minn.*

for the CBS product. The product is shown close up and in use, demonstrating British Telecom's campaign theme, "The world at your fingertips." One of the key communication and design devices is the repeated use of suggestive montages of visual fragments drawn from different flags, countries, currencies, quotations, and urban environments.

This technical section shows not only mastery of telephonic technology but also the sensitivity of the British Telecom's systems

P resto!
Like magic, new cases are entered into Insta-Cite almost as fast as they are issued. Our nearest competitor, Lexis/Auto Cite, is nine to twelve weeks behind.

Surprised? Don't be. For years, Auto-Cite has waited for opinions to be published before they could get them "on-line." WESTLAW's Insta-Cite gets the decisions straight from the judges.

Plus, only WESTLAW's Insta-Cite citation verification/ case history service has an editorial staff of lawyers that keep it up-to-date.

The Insta-Cite staff also insures that every cite, and prior/ subsequent history is complete and accurate.

Insta-Cite is faster and easier to use than Lexis, too. Instant access is direct from any WESTLAW case or case citation.

And cross checking Shepard's citations is done with one simple command.

Insta-Cite.

No one else offers you so much. It's one more reason why those who compare choose the magic of WESTLAW.

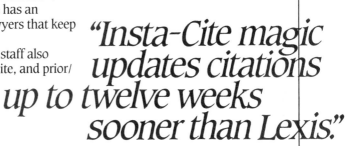

"Insta-Cite magic updates citations up to twelve weeks sooner than Lexis."

and product designers to the changing environment for office auto-mation and advanced financial communications in support of trading. The conceptual and schematic layout of the equipment, consoles, and network architecture is presented on a two-page spread, 70 percent of the way through the brochure. The tactical result is fragmentation of the key appeals just to tell the technical story. Valuable as this is for some readers, the message, design, and placement of these pages, coming at this point in the CBS story, cuts the flow of the dominant

Figure 3.11. The cover of a brochure by British Telecom. *Reprinted by kind permission of British Telecom.*

context of the whole brochure by abruptly shifting gears from the softer, more impressionistic, glamorous themes established earlier. It also serves to isolate a strong sales appeal, which follows it immediately. This kind of material, stressing detailed system features, is out of place in a quasi-documentary brochure because it violates the tone and purpose. In this case there was a solution already in place: the inside back cover of the brochure has a fold-in pocket for extra materials that would have been an excellent place to put the technical description shown above, produced in the form of a folded (unbound) technical supplement. In this manner the needs of the technically oriented reader could have been met without cutting the flow and tone of the overall themes.

IMPLICIT COPY   Production values are high and the photography, typography, technical graphics and printing are of fine quality. A heavy dull-finish coated paper is used that shows the images and type to excellent advantage and has a quality feel and weight. Their effect on the reader is to support the belief that this is indeed an advanced, desirable, powerful, wide ranging and highly sophisticated system.

AUDIENCES   The CBS system is presented in the brochure for the top level manager who makes system wide decisions, a remote buyer. Attention is paid throughout the brochure to the concerns of top management and the system is shown in use by solid-looking professionals in a sophisticated working environment.

EXPLICIT COPY   This brochure is written and produced in a documentary style. The text describes the offerings of InfoLine by listing three business problems that can be addressed on the service: marketing and sales prospecting; finance and credit checking; and corporate intelligence and news. The major print and electronic reference works available on the service are grouped under the appropriate heading to help readers assess their usefulness in their business situation. The vendors who provide the services are named. Search aids and other services are mentioned in a short introduction and again at the end of the book. Customer contact information is provided, along with a phone number. No return card is enclosed.

The prices for online system use are not mentioned anywhere, but free passwords are. There is no attempt to sell the buyer by listing the specific benefits the service delivers to the user, but system features are listed exhaustively throughout.

Behind the screen: unique technology

Central equipment. The size of the central equipment will depend on the particular configuration required by the user, but some examples are given as follows:

System size	Length	Width	Height
10 SCREENS * 90 line	7'6" (1910mm)	2'9" (860mm)	7' (2200mm)
20 SCREENS * 150 line	7'6" (1910mm)	2'9" (860mm)	7' (2200mm)
60 SCREENS * 200 line	10' (3030mm)	2'9" (860mm)	7' (2200mm)

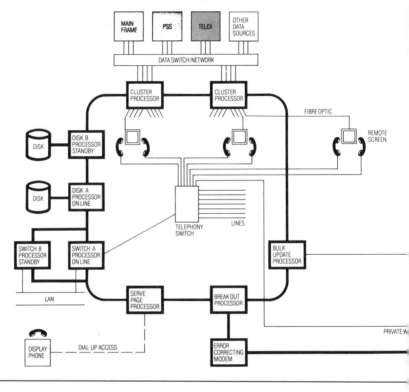

Figure 3.12. A spread from the British Telecom brochure. *Reprinted by kind permission of British Telecom.*

IMPLICIT COPY   There are no images inside the brochure, but the brochure as a whole has a well-mannered, conservative look that becomes a single image. The design and production connote sober quality. The look is pleasantly documentary. There is no "sell" or "pull" to entice the reader into becoming a user of the online system, just an understated explication, the "if-you-know-what-it-is, you'll-definitely-want-it" approach to selling.

The cover attempts to intrigue the reader by using the graphic

The console. The user's console comprises a video monitor with its power supply and a microprocessor control board. The screen is swept by a matrix of infra-red beams giving X-Y co-ordinates. Touching the centre of the key and the consequent breaking of beams identifies the X-Y co-ordinates. This is transmitted to the central equipment which carries out the required transaction.

Network Architecture.
MAIN LOOP. The components of the network are connected to a series of loops. Message packets travel around the main loop with the switch control processor acting as the network control point.

SWITCH PROCESSORS (one on-line and one standby) support both the telephone line scanner and telephone switching matrix (which connects telecom's lines to user handsets). Communications between the switch processor and matrix racks is over a serial data link.

THE DISK PROCESSORS (one on-line and one standby) allow standard computer type access for the other processors on the ring to the 40 MByte Winchester disks. This gives the screen cluster processors access to the stored data pages and the key and short code system files and the switch processor access to required information such as line labels and type of dialling used.

THE CLUSTER PROCESSORS (one per group of up to eight touch sensitive screens) perform the translation between the physical key depression and its designated function – requesting a switching function or displaying another keypage, datapage etc.

Power. The entire system is powered from normal mains supplies. The use of uninterrupted power supplies is also possible as the power consumption is far less than that used by conventional dealing boards with their banks of lights.

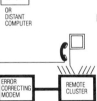

device of redundancy and pattern. The intention of the design is to cause the reader to believe that system is orderly. The color scheme is black with a pattern of repeated red diagonal strokes. The strokes echo and amplify the two double lines in the "N's" of the InfoLine logo. The logo itself is centered in the field of strokes while the title of the brochure is placed at the top of the page in a solid block of red, the color of the strokes. The effect is quiet. The production values are excellent.

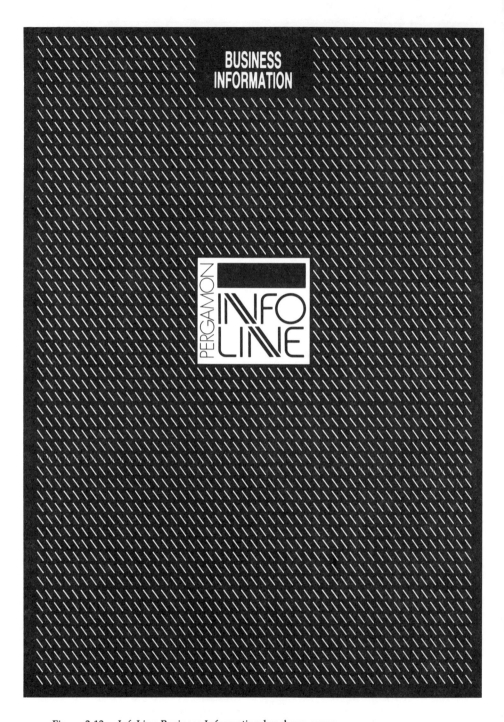

Figure 3.13. InfoLine Business Information brochure cover.

AUDIENCE   The audience is the business community in general. No benefits are cited to engage or interest either the specialist or the nonspecialist, nor is anyone encouraged to be interested in the use or value of the system per se. The audience is bluntly told the features of the system and the general facts of use in a direct fashion.

Archetypes of Brochure Style.

The three brochures can be classified by their dominant styles: fantasy (Westlaw), quasi-documentary (British Telecom Teletrade), and documentary (InfoLine Business Information).

When we compare their communication characteristics the marketing tactics become apparent:

Explicit copy of the brochures

Type	Ideas	Reality	Experience
fantasy	magical or fantasy system	cyberphobic user	user can't handle too much tech or complexity
quasi-docum.	aesthetic/factual	high tech is okay even glamorous	user can do it all, or thinks that he or she can
docum.	plain facts	tech not an issue; content orientation	user is capable of using information technology and understanding its application and potential

Implicit copy of the brochures

Type	Forms	Letters	Colors
fantasy	color illustrations mixed with photos; expressive typography	roman	4-color process
quasi-docum.	factual and expressive photos and illustrations with reserved typography	stylized roman	4-color process
docum.	graphics, no photos, strong text orientation	stylized san serif	2-color

Audiences

Type	Producers	Perceivers	Society
fantasy	marketing	professional end users and users	professional market
quasi-docum.	marketing	top management and endusers	financial market
docum.	marketing	business professionals	general business market

Figure 3.14. Comparison of the uses of three communication variables in the Westlaw, British Telecom Teletrade, and InfoLine Business Information brochures.

From the comparison the general variations permitted by the communication formats for online brochures become clear and a summary of their advantages for marketing can be created:

Fantasy Formats.

Fantasy formats offer the widest context in approaching a subject presumed to be difficult for the reader to accept. The emphasis is on the power of the implicit text. This format is most useful when the marketer is uncertain about the response of the audience to some key aspect of positioning or technology. Its strength is in the work the concept and context do in dealing indirectly with touchy or difficult to resolve emotional issues. It also can achieve high or low entertainment, use playfulness, humor, and visual decoration to keep the faint-hearted reader turning the pages. It allows freedom for striking and unusual presentations of pictorial and text information. Once started, the fantasy theme has to be carried to its conclusion however; it is like a story in the sense that it has to develop the fantasy to involve the reader and then conclude it effectively. If done well, it can strongly differentiate the vendor from the rest of the competititon. If done poorly, it is just a trivial annoyance to the reader.

Quasi-Documentary Formats.

Quasi-documentary formats permit the introduction of glamour into a very limited, mainly fact-oriented, context. The explicit and implicit texts are equally important. Stylish presentation conveys an added value component of high quality and character—a BMW-Rolex-Meridien Hotel look. The fact/glamour balance is hard to sustain in a long publication. Formats over twelve pages need to be written and designed carefully. The shelf life can be limited by changes in style and taste.

Documentary Formats.

Documentary formats are limited to strict information presentations. The emphasis is on the power of the explicit text. They offer little or no contextual entertainment or distraction for the serious reader. They continue to operate well at any length if their typographic variables (legibility and readability) are well calculated and produced. The value added benefits are assumed to be deduced from the facts themselves by the reader. This vanityless approach is highly credible. The result does not have to be visually or textually dull, but substantial wit and professional experience are required to navigate between the florid look and sound of popular science publications on the one side and the stuffy technical report on the other.

Marketing has been shaping these three formats to the various missions requiring brochures. It seems unlikely that any one firm would use all three formats at once or in a single marketing campaign. The positioning of the service determines which format will be most useful and persuasive with the intended buyer and user audiences.

Notes

1. L. Salerno, "What Happened to the Computer Revolution?" *Harvard Business Review* 63, no. 6 (November–December 1985): 137–38.
2. R. Alsop, "Agencies Scrutinize Their Ads for Psychological Symbolism," *Wall Street Journal,* June 11, 1987.
3. N. Baron, "Speech, Sight, and Signs: The Role of Iconicity in Language and Art," *Semiotica* (Amsterdam), 52, nos. 3/4 (1984): 188–212.

4
THE ALL-IMPORTANT SECOND SALE

4.1. Marketing and the Second Sale

If the contract buyer does not use his online service enough, he won't renew. Marketing has to see to it that his system use is both adequate and effective. This kind of use is an important second sale because it is an indirect source of revenue. Mixed pricing strategies make the second sale important because use charges are a source of direct revenue. Marketing tries to keep use at present levels and works on increasing it. The reader can see that marketing is involved in the second sale no matter which pricing schemes are being used.

4.2. The Information Environment

In our complex information environment, user and enduser attitudes toward online systems are formed by coping with the high degree of information noise; enduser feedback; online industry marketing and instructional communications; the user's data research habits and techniques, specifically how the user works with data; and the fact that online systems are high tech products and traditional manual systems aren't.

In this book users are defined as *data workers* and endusers as *information workers:* both are *knowledge workers.* Human beings doing knowledge work in the real world are infinitely more complicated, handsome, and imaginative than these definitions suggest, but the definitions are modeled on a powerful and important distinction that Theodore Levitt, Edward W. Carter Professor of business administration at the Harvard Business School draws between data and information: Levitt writes, "The difference between data and information is that while data are endlessly aggregated collections of raw facts, information represents the selective organization and imaginative interpretation of those facts. This requires knowing, in some sort of direct and systematic way, the world with which one presumes to deal."[1]

KNOWLEDGE WORKERS

The definitions of knowledge workers listed below follow directly from the relationship of source research to the world's need for information and knowledge. Knowledge workers are categorized by their knowledge of sources, or of the world, or by the way in which they interact with data or information:

1. Users who perform searches for subsequent analysis are sometimes endusers, too; more often their activities support and feed into the analysis of others. Users organize, collect, and report.
2. Endusers, those who add new value to data by either accepting them as valid information or changing them into information, and who, therefore, have a research need, are consumers of online searches, and are sometimes contributors to the databases and other sources of data.

Functional analysis suggests that the user and the enduser require separate marketing programs because they play different roles in their organizations and the world; in particular, they are getting different benefits from the same database products and interact differently with same data. A contrast and comparison of their interactions with the operations, output, and other characteristics of online systems shows two consistent sets of online marketing variables.

USER   Values the technology of online systems for its ease of use and productivity during searching.

ENDUSER   Values the output of online searching over the technology of searching, may even be indifferent to the technology used.

USER   Is focused on the research and data needs of his search activity initiator, the enduser.

ENDUSER   Is focused on the world-related needs of the end consumer of information, the information activity initiator.

USER   Interacts actively with the search material by finding, collecting, and collating. Is reporting oriented and values thoroughness.

ENDUSER   Interacts actively with the search data by transforming it into information. Values cogent answers to his questions.

USER   Collects and organizes search data from all available sources.

ENDUSER   Matches, analyzes, and synthesizes search data against the needs of the world.

USER   Is set in motion by the enduser.

ENDUSER   Is set in motion by the endconsumer of information.

USER   Relates tactically to the search issues.

ENDUSER   Operates strategically and tactically on the search and research issues, and operationally on the assessment, formation, and distribution of cogent information.

Users and endusers have widely varying capabilities and interests. Some will fit the descriptions on the list above, others will never fit on any list because of their creativity, imagination, and skill. If every sales call in the online industry could be made by a salesperson who could estimate the character and training of the individuals involved, there would be little need for the mass communications and mass marketing techniques that use these kinds of definitions.

4.3. Major User and Enduser Markets

PROFESSIONALS AND THEIR ALLIED ORGANIZATIONS

The growth of online databases for the professions has been dramatic and profitable. Law, medicine, engineering, accounting, and finance are natural marketing targets. Each area of professional practice is based on a specific body of knowledge with its use in its market controlled by a licensing system designed to assure a minimum quality of professional performance. To a greater or lesser degree all professions have a tradition of research performed on behalf of their clients. In many cases the client pays directly for all or some of the time and materials used in research. In other instances the research cost is supported by the government or by public and private institutions. Automating some aspects of the research process means that all professionals do their searches better, faster, easier, or more competitively.

A hotly debated question in online marketing is whether law partners, doctors, senior CPA's, etc., actually use the databases themselves or have the task assigned to someone else. The industry is too new for anyone to know for sure what these endusers are doing and what the stable long-term patterns will be. It is safe to assume that more associates are using online databases than principals are at this time. The reason is billable staff expense. Cost is not the only factor determining patterns of use; many professionals continue to be intimidated by computers and online systems. Some are truly cyberphobic, while many can't afford to use their time in this manner or find the technology distasteful.

Specialists in the professions will have lower needs for online databases than will generalists. To the generalist the database is a special boon. The specialist usually follows one or two well-known paths mainly to find the latest data (he or she has mastered the rest). The generalist, of necessity, is not as well informed on all the details of a given question; therefore, his or her penetration into a database may be deeper, more frequent, and more wide ranging. In both cases the use of an online database is often a preliminary step in the decision-making process leading to full-scale research in a library or laboratory, or to facilitate directing the library or bench research of others.

DECISION MAKERS—EXECUTIVES, SENIOR SCIENTISTS, ETC.—AND THEIR ALLIED ORGANIZATIONS

Like professionals, executives initiate and are confronted by questions whose solutions can often be supported by online searching. The job of the executive is to productively direct the work of others. The executive, therefore, has a work-related mission in knowing how to direct online searches. More executives are going online themselves as computerization spreads in the executive suite.

Marketing strategies for the decision-maker will have to follow the track of the slowly rising computer installation and office automation curves. The reader will have to make up his own mind, but I believe that decision makers as a class are increasingly aware of electronic databases and the value of online services. Whether or not they choose to use them at this time cannot be assumed to be based completely on a lack of awareness of the value and uses of the services.

Too many social, technical, and economic variables are at work in these decisions for anyone to be able to center on any one issue, but a recent study of corporations showed that while the most frequent applications performed on corporate microcomputer systems were spread-sheets, word processing, database management, and planning, nearly 40 percent used their computers for outside database access and 36 percent used electronic mail.

The combined current and projected use of online databases as projected by the corporations themselves is at 85 percent for all business users of microcomputers. Current "computerization" of top management is about 20 percent; over the next five years the percentage is expected to rise to 60 percent. Some observers argue that computer installations do not accumulate into online markets, that this idea is a myth having little to do with the future growth of the online industry. Regardless of the reasoning behind this claim, the computer market studies indicate that awareness of online services and a growing demand for online databases is a purchase factor in computer sales. The author interprets these data as an indicator of a major marketing opportunity, suggesting that the direct use of online databases by executives and decision makers will probably increase significantly in the years ahead because of trends in office automation and corporate decentralization (e.g., among the Fortune 2000 companies, access to outside databases accounted for 39 percent of the uses of installed microcomputers, with 46 percent projecting database access as one of the prime uses of all systems).[2] Much of this opportunity can be wasted unless (1) it is declared a market opportunity, (2) proactive marketing is applied to the opportunity, and (3) marketing intensity increases as the installation curve rises.

4.4. Major User Market Segments

LIBRARIANS AND THEIR ALLIED KNOWLEDGE ORGANIZATIONS

This segment is composed of full- and part-time knowledge workers and volunteers who, when compared by their training levels and systems knowledge to those of professionals and executives, are "professional" users of online systems. Marketing must take their database fluency into account. Marketing must also be aware that price elasticity is low and price sensitivity is high in this market because of widely held beliefs about the right of the public to free or low cost information. Many librarians feel threatened by the incursion of online services and the spread of enduser searching in the institutions and intellectual communities they serve. Marketing must recognize this sensitivity for what it is and deal with it in marketing programs addressed separately to the librarian and the user.

RESEARCHERS, SCIENTISTS, JOURNALISTS, ETC., AND THEIR ALLIED KNOWLEDGE ORGANIZATIONS

This segment is composed of full- and part-time knowledge workers who need answers to questions posed by others or who generate systematic inquiries related to their own work. These workers are often skillful users of database systems and all other knowledge resources. They are often contributors to the databases they use. Marketing will respond to their expertise by influencing product design to allow them to do what they need.

ADVISORS, COMMUNICATORS, AND CONSULTANTS

In accepting assignments to be solved on their clients' behalf, many advisors, communicators, and consultants have become excellent and frequent databases users. While price elasticity is high and sensitivity is low in this group, marketing must recognize that its search opportunities are time/cost constrained. System pricing, speed, and accuracy, therefore, are major factors in persuasive communications. Also, these knowledge workers are almost universally endusers, translating their searches into information for their clients, the endconsumers of information. Marketing should stress the low cost of conversion of online data into information where possible.

SECOND-LEVEL KNOWLEDGE WORKERS— PARAPROFESSIONALS, ADMINISTRATIVE ASSOCIATES, AND SECRETARIES

I believe that these knowledge workers form a large body of users, especially in business. Owing to corporate paranoia and the need that some executives have to cloak all of their activities with an artificial secrecy designed to inflate their value to others, many data collection assignments are given to the closest trusted person or reliable direct report, and not to the most skillful online user or general researcher in the organization. Many of those chosen are well informed in a narrow sense on the issues they are asked to search. Many may have a good feel for the amount and kinds of data needed in the situation at hand. Second-level knowledge workers are superficially cheaper to use than knowledge professionals, and often quite effective or lucky. If future user studies should happen to confirm this impression, marketing could take a special interest in this segment of users. Products could be simplified to meet their needs and operator and pricing materials could be reconfigured to meet their task interests and need for secrecy.

STUDENTS

In the professional schools many students are alloted free use of the specialized online systems that support their future professions. This form of study aids their learning and topic mastery, makes the school seem progressive, and seemingly encourages acceptance and use of online systems by the professions. Most of these programs are sponsored and well supported by marketing. The verdict is not in on their long-term effectiveness in encouraging specific brand loyalty and online use after graduation.

HACKERS

Professionals, executives, librarians, and so on are mainly interested in online information as an exchange utility in their work for endusers or endconsumers. Hackers are interested in online information systems as communication and technical processes and structures. While their contribution to the technology and communication climate is undeniably valuable, thrill-seeking "segments" are too small to command marketing involvement, with the exception of the gateway services where SIG's have been formed. This may be a growth market for all services, however, and should be monitored closely by marketing.

TOURISTS

There is an unknown number of "tourists," "curiosity seekers," and "barracks lawyers" of all types using online services to some extent every day. They do not constitute a homogeneous market segment but, like hackers, they are a weak force to be watched.

HOME USERS

It is too early to know what the home user will do with online databases. Much depends on the success of the computer industry in solving their marketing, technical, and service problems, and on the online industries' interest and effectiveness in solving ease-of-use problems for the unsupported user. I believe that as online use spreads in organizational and institutional settings, many will bring the habit home and spread use to others in their families and among their acquaintances. If my intuition is borne out, marketers may well find that their marketing efforts in the major markets cover the potential home user market quite well, and that special marketing programs would be redundant. The situation bears close watching to see what should be done, if anything. The emotional values of buyers in the home market segments would differ widely. MBA's, librarians, and research directors, for example, are very different cats at work and at home. Imaginative marketers could classify customers into segments by their characteristic demographics and psychographics, as is done in other household-oriented marketing programs.

SATISFACTION IN THE ACT OF ONLINE SEARCHING FROM THE USER'S POINT OF VIEW

Marketing managers, sales people, and user research all agree that the highest satisfaction the user obtains from online searching occurs when the enduser of the data conducts a successful search himself. The pleasure is in the interactions that yield answers—process rewards. Assigning the task to another diminishes the process reward.

4.5. Marketing Communications in the Second Sale

The user materials examined below are exampleS of how one user-oriented online organization has built a consistent document system in support of its marketing goals. The examples are created and used by The Source, whose marketing is aimed exclusively at the user. It is important for the reader to keep in mind that The Source is an *information utility*, a term they coined themselves, with a subscriber base of about 80,000. An information utility provides more to its users. As its name implies, it also provides telecommunications services and

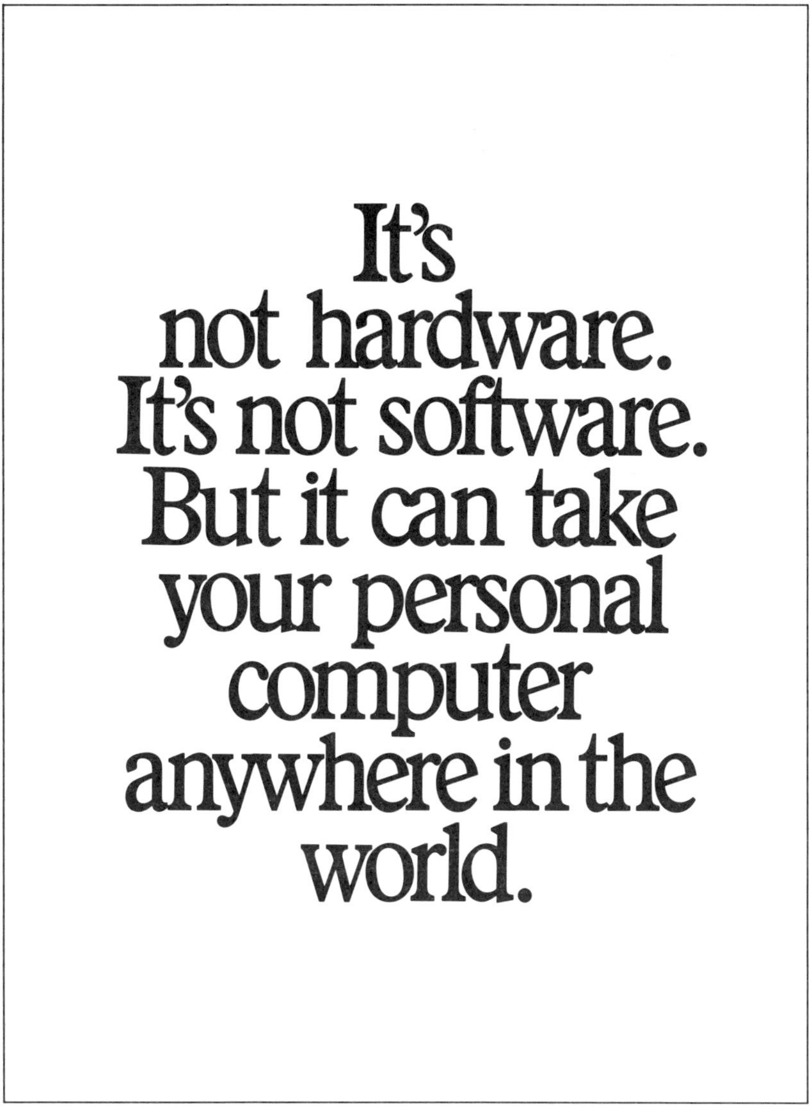

It's not hardware. It's not software. But it can take your personal computer anywhere in the world.

Figure 4.1. The Source brochure: size 8 ½ × 11 inches.

timely information. The marketing campaign of The Source is focused on the user because of its variable pricing approach. (It has a low subscription fee and its revenue comes from variable charges.) User focus makes this material useful for study and sheds light on the subsequent marketing and communication choices.

Inclusion here is not an endorsement of The Source or of its

Figure 4.2. The Source brochure (second spread): size 11 × 17 inches.

approach to these issues; the examples below are evidence of its carefully planned user campaign and it is presented here for the reader's benefit, as are all of the examples in this book. A study of one literature system has the advantage of allowing the reader to examine the degree of unity and follow-through required in the conception, text, and art in a whole user program. (Space considerations will not permit reviews of several systems and a comparison of them as has been done elsewhere in this book.) The reader however can make some limited judgments about the numerous marketing, design, and communication issues affecting all marketing communications for users. Another reason for choosing The Source's materials is that it ranks in the low-to-middle interval in production value and overall expense. The reader can see that modestly handsome and effective user communications for a large mixed audience of users can be created and prepared on a relatively small budget.

Note: the definitions used in the analysis of marketing communications examples are:

Explicit copy.   The reality and experience that we use words and pictures to describe in marketing communications, usually the marketing message to the buyer audience.

Implicit copy.   The meanings that arise from the combinations of words, shapes, sizes, physical arrangement, styles, colors, and technical details of marketing communications.

Audiences.   Those who produce the marketing communications, those who are the market targets of the producers, and all of those audiences who may be addressed indirectly or who may comprehend the market communication.

All of the visual examples in this section are copyrighted 1987 by Source Telecomputing Corporation. All rights are reserved.

DOCUMENT.   The Omnibus brochure. This brochure is prepared in quasi-documentary format. The production is in two colors, red and black, on slick, folded white paper. When the reader first encounters it, it is folded down to 8 1/2 × 11 inches in size. It can be opened to 11 × 17 inches and then to 22 x 17 inches. These mechanical changes in format give a sense of progressive revelation; the reader is engaged by the text as the physical and visual effect increases.

EXPLICIT COPY.   This spread, figure 4.2, introduces the system and the service. The Source is an information reference/delivery/transmission system, all in one. The service is obtained by the user through his PC. The Source is presented as a utility that adds value to PC investments (which are viewed as not paying off). This is a way of overcoming cyberphobic resistance by directing the attention of the reader to a more acceptable or comfortable issue. It is also a strong value-added reason for subscription even if one is satisfied with his PC. The Source's text points to two levels of content: business or factual, and pleasurable.

EXPLICIT COPY. This spread, figure 4.3, is about benefits of the service, many of which are reviewed in detail and some of which are visualized for the reader.

IMPLICIT COPY. The typography and pictures are of solid quality and affect the reader because they fit legibly into the changing scales and sensations of the layout. Boldness is effectively used in key lines of type and the color red, used in other type areas, creates an alternating rhythmic visual tempo throughout the piece. The pictures are clear and relevant and avoid showing the features of the system in favor of a home terminal in use or one fully integrated into office and other settings. As the pages unfold the text deepens in the variety of its arguments and the length of the text presented in support of the arguments increases, drawing the reader in further. The quality of the printing is fine and the paper is of high quality.

AUDIENCES Organizations and individuals are addressed simultaneously as endusers, users, and initial buyers in the text. The marketing plan pivots on the PC itself and its productivity. Since The Source assumes that the PC is common to all prospect groups, the complexity of shaping the appeals to the individual information and social needs and interests of the various audiences can be minimized. The marketing edge of this tactic is its relative universality.

DOCUMENT The membership agreement is a rather lighthearted financial document that plays with looking serious. The effect keeps the act of joining in a clever perspective. The production quality is high, and the value of the document to the whole presentation can't be overestimated.

DOCUMENT The rate and fee card is clear and concise. The rates (potential billable charges for use) are demystified. The size of the card is such that it makes a good reference document to keep near the PC.

Figure 4.3. The Source brochure (internal spread): size 17 × 22 inches.

DOCUMENT   The command guide is, like the other materials, direct and simple to read and use. It is three-ring punched for inclusion in The Source operator's manual. Its small size lends itself well to fitting into a brief case or purse, as does the rate card. Throughout attention has been paid to use and practicality.

DOCUMENT   *SourceWorld* magazine is an 8 1/2 × 11-inch occasional magazine for Source users. It features high-spirited editorial

matter and uses cartoons to make its point. It is an easy read. The production values of *SourceWorld* are high—it is the most complexly designed and printed piece in the all-inclusive omnibus kit folders that The Source sends out.

DOCUMENT   Cover Letter to the customer.

TECHNICAL ITEM   United States postage paid return envelope.

MEMBERSHIP AGREEMENT

SOURCE TELECOMPUTING CORPORATION
1616 Anderson Road   McLean, Virginia 22102
(703) 734-7500

Authorization

I hereby authorize Source Telecomputing Corp-oration to charge all costs I incur as a member of THE SOURCE, including usage, storage and monthly minimum, directly to the credit card, purchase order or business account indicated, unless I otherwise notify STC in writing. I represent that I am 21 years of age or older. I have read and agree to all of the terms and conditions stated on the back of this Agreement, and I agree that those terms state my complete membership rights.

___/___/___
Date   Member's Signature

PLEASE PRINT YOUR NAME AND ADDRESS

Name _____

Organization Name (if membership is for business use) _____

Address _____

City_____ State____ Zip_____

Country (if not U.S.) _____

Telephone Work (____)_____

Telephone Home (____)_____

Mother's maiden name for verification (if password lost) _____

PLEASE MAIL THIS AGREEMENT TO THE SOURCE WITHIN 10 DAYS. USAGE OF YOUR ACCOUNT CON-STITUTES ACCEPTANCE OF MEMBERSHIP TERMS AND CONDITIONS.

Your Membership Entitles You to:

- Access to the many services of THE SOURCE.
- THE SOURCE Manual.
- Personal Membership Card for your ID Number and Password.
- THE SOURCE Command Guide.
- Simple Sign-On instructions.
- Customer Support Services.

Membership Terms

PLEASE CHECK ONE BOX:

CREDIT CARD BILLING
☐ Please bill my credit card for monthly charges.

DIRECT BILLING (BUSINESS USE ONLY)
☐ Please bill my organization for monthly charges, sub-ject to initial credit approval. (If your organization re-quires a purchase order, one must be enclosed with this Agreement.)

SEE THE ENCLOSED RATES AND FEES SCHEDULE FOR ALL CHARGES. PAYMENTS MUST BE IN U.S. DOLLARS.

Credit Card: ☐ VISA ☐ MasterCard ☐ American Express

Number:
| | | | | | | | | | | | | | | | | | |

Expiration Date: ___/___/___

What EQUIPMENT will you use with THE SOURCE?

_____
Manufacturer & Model

☐ CHECK HERE IF YOU HAVE RECEIVED YOUR ID NUMBER OVER THE PHONE AND INDICATE NUMBER BELOW. (DO NOT SEND US YOUR PASSWORD)

ID No._____

Password _____

Host System No. _____

Date Assigned _____

0004-7 B

Figure 4.4. The Source membership agreement: one of two similar carbonless pages.

HOURS OF OPERATION

The Source services are available 24 hours a day, 7 days a week.

PRIME TIME . . . 7AM to 6PM, your local time, Monday-Friday

NON-PRIME TIME . . . 6PM to 7AM, your local time, Monday-Friday, all day Saturday, Sunday and holidays (New Year's Day, July 4th, Labor Day, Thanksgiving Day and Christmas Day)

The Source may be temporarily unavailable due to maintenance between 4-6AM, Eastern Time. For areas without daylight savings time: from the last Sunday of April to the last Sunday of October, Prime Time hours are 6AM to 5PM, your local time.

REGISTRATION

The suggested retail price for the one-time registration fee to The Source is $49.95, plus $3 postage/handling in the U.S. and Canada. ($15 postage/handling outside the U.S. and Canada)

MEMBERSHIP

There is a $10 monthly Membership Fee which is credited toward your monthly usage of The Source.

Members may pay a one- or two-year Annual Membership Fee rather than the $10 monthly fee. Paying a one-year Membership Fee of $95 saves you $25; a two-year fee of $175 saves you $65. To apply for the program, send SourceMail to TCA068 or call Customer Support at 800/336-3330 (from Virginia and outside the continental U.S., call 703/821-8888).

FREE ONLINE SERVICES

Certain services on The Source are available to members free of online charges. These are noted online and in documentation and include the Tutorial <TUTOR>; Member Information <INFO>; Introduction <INTRO>; Billing and Usage Information <DETAIL>; and Rates and Storage Fees <RATES>. You can also send free SourceMail to Billing by typing DETAIL 3 at Command Level and to Customer Support by typing SUPPORT at Command Level. Please note that any extra telecommunications fees you may pay are charged on these services.

BASIC USAGE

THE SOURCE USAGE COST/MINUTE	300 BAUD	1200 BAUD	2400 BAUD
Standard Services			
Prime Time	.36	.43	.46
Non-Prime Time	.14	.18	.20
Special Interest Groups (SIGS)			

These discounted rates apply when using most of the Special Interest Groups services available on The Source.

	300 BAUD	1200 BAUD	2400 BAUD
Prime Time	.18	.23	.25
Non-Prime Time	.10	.13	.15

CHAT

These rates apply when using CHAT on The Source. There is no baud surcharge for CHAT.

	300 BAUD	1200 BAUD	2400 BAUD
Prime Time	.36	.36	.36
Non-Prime Time	.14	.14	.14

Figure 4.5. The Source rate card.

INFORMATION NETWORK

•The Source℠

Command
Guide
1986

Including
New
Special Interest
Groups!

Figure 4.6.   The Source command guide.

TECHNICAL ITEM   Each of the above brochures can be delivered to the prospect as part of an omnibus information kit folder (OIKF). OIKF's are in widespread use in high tech industries. Their practicality and relative economy is undeniable, but their overall composition and ultimate marketing effect on the prospective buyer is open to serious discussion. We will examine The Source's OKIF in detail.

SUMMARY OF THE SOURCE'S OIKF   The reader will have noticed the consistent visual image of The Source's materials. Regularly repeated typographic elements have been used throughout. Graphics and text style give these materials a corporate and product identity regardless of the quality of the reproduction. The clarity of the text is exceptional and reassuring to the reader. The whole package suggests that using The Source may be exactly the same kind of experience as reading its materials—practical and content laden, but with a modest touch of style and good humor. The positioning is engaging and could be summed up as: we have what you want (or you can create what you want for yourself and others) be it serious or fun; but we don't take ourselves too seriously, we aren't stuffy.

This OIKF package is successful at the buyer level. Despite its length (eighty-nine pages) and the number of documents included (nineteen) it remains inviting, readable, and consistent with The Source style. It communicates pertinently about The Source and its products. It speaks well for the company in its judicious combination of economy in documents where it doesn't matter and expenditure on documents that count. It is a model of clarity and demystification. It instills and maintains a memorable impression of quality.

Most OIKF's in the online industry are produced in the form of a two-pocket folder large enough to hold a lot of 8 1/2 × 11-inch printed information. The one we will examine is mailed by The Source in response to prospective buyer inquiries.

JUNE/JULY 1987

The Source is entering an exciting, high-growth era. Major new services have been introduced. Others have been significantly improved. And, as you read the following pages, remember—this is only the beginning!

The all new APPLE Special Interest Group rewards you with high-quality software for downloading, quick answers to your computing questions, and a newly designed menu and file library. Sophisticated, yet easy-to-use, new financial databases help take the guesswork out of your stock and mutual fund investments. New EXCHANGES offer you decision-support through conferences, workshops, and reference libraries—all in one. Twelve enhanced bulletin boards offer you the industry's most-wanted features. A renewed Microsearch™ fulfills its promise as your definitive source of hardware and software product information.

Still, our commitment to you doesn't stop with new and improved services. You get the most from The Source with a FREE APPLESIG tool kit, complete with downloading utilities and user guides; a FREE Microsearch thesaurus, a valuable online time-saver; and a FREE poster attractively displaying all major menus at-a-glance. And, remember, "this is only the beginning."

What's Inside:
- New APPLESIG 2
- Improved Microsearch 2
- ButtonWare Support in IBMSIG . . . 3
- New Vestor Stock Screening 4
- New CDA Analysis 5
- New Exchanges 6
- New POST PLUS 7
- New MEDSIG 7
- FREE Menu Map 8

Figure 4.7. *SourceWorld* magazine: cover page.

The Source
INFORMATION NETWORK
®

Welcome Online!

We cordially welcome you as one of the newest members of The Source. We've compiled many of the industry's finest databases and communication services to meet your business and personal computing needs.

You'll get inexpensive software and quick answers to computing questions in Special Interest Groups. Locate profitable investments with a full range of financial databases. Transmit messages cross-country in minutes with acclaimed mail and conferencing services. Be among the first to know what's happening locally and around the globe with up-to-the-minute news services -- and much more!

The enclosed Kit provides everything you need to begin using The Source right now. But first, please take a few minutes to:

o **learn how to save 27%** on your use of The Source by reading the "Billing Options" Card in the front flap of your kit.

o **sign and return your New Member Validation Card** to assure that you'll receive announcements of new products, discounts, and more!

o **locate your ID and password.** Please transfer your password to a private place and protect it as you would your credit card.

o **use The Source Directory** to find out all that's online and waiting for you. Become an expert navigator with our menu map of services.

o **take your turn with The Source Tutor,** your FREE online guided tour of The Source. Select option #1 on the introductory menu.

Better yet, The Source offers the **best support in the industry and it's FREE!** Have questions about setting up your modem and software? About specific services on The Source? Call us toll-free at 800-336-3330 (703-821-8888 in Virginia or outside the continental U.S.) or send us a free message via The Source. Simply select MEMBER INFORMATION off of the introductory menu.

We are extremely pleased that you have chosen The Source as your online service -- communicate with us often. Let us know how we can continue to serve you with the best quality product possible.

Sincerely,

J.J. Davidson
The Source

P.S. Please send us your New Member Validation Card within the next 5 days. We've paid the postage so you can simply drop it in the mail. Remember: Your account has been assigned and your $10 monthly membership fee will soon be in effect.

1616 Anderson Road, McLean, Virginia 22102 703/734-7500

The Source is a registered service mark of Source Telecomputing Corporation.

Figure 4.8.   A customer letter from The Source.

Figure 4.9.   The Source return envelope.

INFORMATION KIT

Figure 4.10.   The Source omnibus information kit folder (OKIF).

TECHNICAL FEATURE The left-hand pocket contains sales and buyer contact materials.

CONTENT	PAGES	PRODUCTION	QUALITY		
1. Letter to prospect	1	typed, signed	M		
2. Brochure	8	2 color, printed		H	
3. Postpaid envelope	1	printed	M		
4. Contract	2	printed		H	
5. Welcome to The Source	20	photocopy			L
6. Private network	7	photocopy			L
7. Private networks	7	photocopy			L
TOTALS	46	7 pieces	3	2	2

Figure 4.11. The contents of the left-hand pocket of The Source's OKIF.

TECHNICAL FEATURE The right-hand pocket contains technical, operational support, and after-sale support materials.

CONTENTS	PAGES	PRODUCTION TYPE	QUALITY		
1. Rate and fee card	2	printing	M		
2. Command guide	20	printing	M		
3. advertisement reprint	1	printing	M		
4. *SourceWorld* magazine	4	printing		H	
5. fact sheet	2	photocopy			L
6. press release	2	photocopy			L
7. press release	5	photocopy			L
8. 12 articles	5	photocopy			L
TOTALS	41	12 pieces	8	3	1

Figure 4.12. The contents of the right-hand pocket of The Source's OKIF.

OIKF Eighty-seven pages, in nineteen bindings.

SUMMARY OF THE CONTENTS OF BOTH POCKETS		
LEFT	RIGHT	OKF TOTALS
7 pieces	12 pieces	19 pieces
(46 pages)	(41 pages)	(87 pages)
3 LOW: 4 M & H	8 LOW: 4 M & H	11 LOW: 7 M & H

Figure 4.13. Summary of the contents of The Source's OKIF.

IMPRESSION OF THE OIKF   The production values of the folder itself are quite high and this quality establishes a level that colors the whole presentation. This is critical because 63 percent of the presentation is poorly designed and cheaply produced photocopied material. The folder is a value-enhancing context in which the lesser materials are automatically valued more highly.

DOCUMENTS IN THE OIKF   If the folder establishes the quality image, and 63 percent of the materials are of low quality, how does an impression of quality persist after the folder has been opened? The answer is that the important, must-read documents are produced at medium or high quality while all of the low-quality materials are optional reading. Production quality signifies to the reader those documents that should be read first and those that are optional, secondary, or unimportant. The high quality documents form a rich quality stratum in the presentation: they are the letter, the omnibus brochure, the contract, and a copy of *SourceWorld* magazine. The highly structured main sales pathway runs directly through these documents. If they were all read one would get the full sales pitch. All of the other documents support the case for subscription but from many different points of view. They form an unstructured series of pathways leading back to the main sales pathway.

COST OF THE OIKF   Is it necessary to send so much to the potential client? If the prospect is unqualified prior to mailing, sending the whole packet may be the best choice because the information needs of the buyer can't be predicted. If the client is qualified prior to mailing, sending more pointed materials and a smaller quantity of material is more cost and sales efficient.

IMPRESSION OF THE OIKF'S MATERIALS   At another level altogether the sheer quantity of material suggests the abundance and importance of research data that can be obtained from The Source's databases by online searching. Its mass implies information in bulk; its quality and manageability implies the operational characteristics of the systems.

DOCUMENT   Subscriber mailings. Here is the front of a "new customer" card from The Source.

EXPLICIT COPY   The image of a tandem bike of infinite length is a symbol for The Source and one with pleasurable associations for most readers.

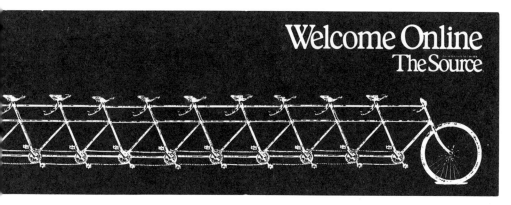

Figure 4.14.   The Source's "new customer" card: side one.

Dear New Member,

re very pleased to welcome you to The Source.
help you get started, here are some services you'll want to try right away.

Command
Level, type: For:

TOR ....A guided tour of the most popular services on The Source—free of
online charges.

?O ....Account and billing information new members find helpful. Plus a list of the
most frequently-asked questions & answers.

MBERS ....To list yourself in the online Member Directory.

GGEST ....To send suggestions to The Source.

TAIL ....Your past month's charges are put online about the 15th of every month.

Of course, you may call our Customer Support Department at (800) 336-3330, here to
ve you 7 days a week, 17 hours each day. (In Virginia and outside the U.S. call 703/821-
8.) Or, contact us by sending SourceMail to TCA088. (Type **MAIL S TCA088** at
nmand Level.) Our Customer Support Department will send the answers back to you via SourceMail.

And remember to change your password regularly. It takes just seconds. Type **CPW** at
Command Level and follow the prompts. Don't give your password to others who should
not have access to your account; you are responsible for all usage charges to your account.

Please take a moment to verify your address and billing information. If there are any
errors, call our Billing Department at (703) 734-7500 or send a SourceMail message by
typing **DETAIL 3** at Command Level. (There are no online charges for contacting the
Billing Department electronically via The Source.)

Thank you for joining The Source. We look forward to serving you in the months ahead.

Sincerely,

Sharon Hox
Vice President
Customer Services

Figure 4.15.   The Source's "new customer" card: inside of card (with signature).

IMPLICIT COPY   The colors of the card are peppy and fun. The inside of the card gives tips on use and other pertinent information designed to get the new subscriber on the system fast. The text is chatty and casual and the card is personalized with a signature.

EXPLICIT COPY   This is a clear, easy to read layout, figure 4.16, depicting the services available at The Source. Its layout follows the organization of the user's manual itself and presents the highlights and command names of the various subsections of the services.

IMPLICIT COPY   The posterlike format is attractive, memorable, and well organized for quick reference and double checking. It is

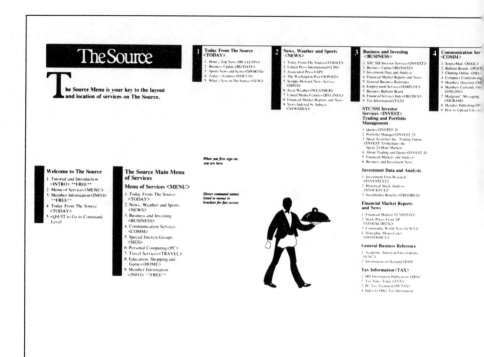

Figure 4.16. The Source's "new customer" menu: side one.

scaled to fit in The Source manual and does so in a usable way. The spirited colors and graphics set a mood for the otherwise too dry data that makes the reader more interested in reading the list. This inviting approach is useful in getting the complex messages read and accepted by the user.

4.6. SIMPLICITY IN USER MATERIALS

Collectively, The Source, CompuServe, and Dow Jones News retrieval companies have a United States user base approaching a million. They are doing something right as far as the user is concerned. Part of that is creating clear, concise, and easy to use materials. Since they all deal with large, highly diverse user markets, their materials demonstrate a concerted attempt in the United States online industry to find a common communication and marketing ground with their user market.

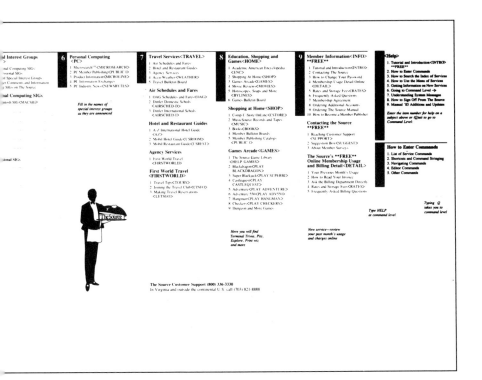

The straightforward quality of the materials reviewed here may have come about partly because the information utilities are not dealing in specialized services like medicine or law where the nature of the searches is complex indeed. Partly it comes from their pricing simplicity, which makes their selling easier.

It seems more likely to me however that information utilities are user oriented to a degree that the specialized services have yet to attain. Part of it comes from (1) the marketing clarity mandated by pricing, (2) the business and marketing intuition that information utilities have to be easy to use or they will fail, and (3) the utilities' marketing, commercial, and philosophical history. Whatever the source of the marketing inspiration is, there is something to be said for any approach that successfully gathers tens of thousands of users at their terminals each day and makes searching an easy and pleasurable activity for most of them. I hope that the lessons to be learned from their directness and simplicity are not lost on the other services.

Figure 4.17. The Source's "new customer" menu: cover.

4.7. Marketing and the User Manual

One last example will be examined from The Source's document set, The Source manual.

DOCUMENT   User's manual.

EXPLICIT COPY   From the cover to the last insert page the quality of The Source's manual is consistent with all of the other materials in their marketing communication system. The presentation of the data is both clear and direct. The operations data are easy to follow, and commands are presented in legible routines with defined notes and activity prompts.

IMPLICIT COPY   It fits comfortably on a bookstand or desktop, and the ring binding is designed so that the small pages can be turned easily with a minimum of physical damage. Tab dividers group the major subsections for easy reference. This layout is part of a risk-reduction approach to user comfort, although I doubt if it was conceived in exactly that way by the manual's authors.

USER DOCUMENT   Getting started. In The Source manual the first section, called "Getting started," covers basic equipment issues, access to The Source, use of the manual, basic commands, membership ethics and protocols, customer support, billing, and the sign-on procedure. This chapter is directed at reducing the initial nervousness of the user to manageable proportions and establishing a comfortable pathway for gaining access that is somewhat free from mystery and self-doubt. The hidden assumption is that an increased degree of user confidence will permit a higher degree of price risk. The rest of the manual teaches how to manage the risk of use (not price risk) for each facet of the service.

USER DOCUMENTS   Command guide pages 18–19.

USER DOCUMENTS   Business and investment section, pages 54–55.

USER DOCUMENTS   News, weather, and sports section, pages 16–17.

USER DOCUMENTS   Communication services, pages 20–21.

USER DOCUMENTS   Travel services, pages 8–9.

Figure 4.18. The Source manual slip cover.

Figure 4.19. The Source manual cover.

THE SOURCE MANUAL

Getting Started

Getting Started 1

Figure 4.20. The Source page: getting started.

The Source®
New Member
Kit

We're changing the way
you work and play

Figure 4.21.   The Source publication: *The Source New Member Kit*.

COMMENT ON USER DOCUMENTS FROM THE SOURCE

The Source has been careful to make the whole process of buying and using an online service as clear and humane as possible; a "face," if you will, has been put on the usually "faceless" paperwork used in sales and communication, and stamped on the electronic searching process itself, as it is encountered and guided by the manual. The Source has succeeded in getting its manual to look and feel like all of its other materials. The same quality strategy is followed throughout—each document communicates and restates the same underlying message of clarity and friendliness by its modest quality, sober usability, and a certain lightheartedness that bubbles like a brook through the whole literature system.

The Source has a marketing identity that it uses in everything it prints. Taken individually, the manual and other documents look about like all of the rest of the online industry's work. When they are

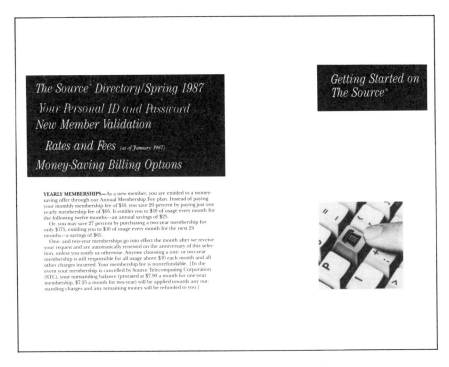

The Source® Directory/Spring 1987

Your Personal ID and Password

New Member Validation

Rates and Fees (as of January 1987)

Money-Saving Billing Options

Getting Started on The Source®

YEARLY MEMBERSHIPS—As a new member, you are entitled to a money-saving offer through our Annual Membership Fee plan. Instead of paying your monthly membership fee of $10, you save 20 percent by paying just one yearly membership fee of $95. It entitles you to $10 of usage every month for the following twelve months—an annual savings of $25.

Or, you may save 27 percent by purchasing a two-year membership for only $175, entitling you to $10 of usage every month for the next 24 months—a savings of $65.

One- and two-year memberships go into effect the month after we receive your request and are automatically renewed on the anniversary of this selection, unless you notify us otherwise. Anyone choosing a one- or two-year membership is still responsible for all usage above $10 each month and all other charges incurred. Your membership fee is nonrefundable. [In the event your membership is cancelled by Source Telecomputing Corporation (STC), your outstanding balance (prorated at $7.90 a month for one-year membership, $7.25 a month for two-year) will be applied towards any outstanding charges and any remaining money will be refunded to you.]

Figure 4.22. "Getting Started on the Source" from *The Source New Member Kit*.

reviewed in the manner used here, the reader can see the full effect on the buyer and user of exposure to consistently applied and executed marketing, quality control, and communications tactics. Consistency and conceptual excellence in marketing and marketing communications are shown to be good bedfellows.

4.8. The User Manual
MISSIONS

The manual is for the person who actually puts his fingers on the keys and operates the system. The user has conflicting needs for manuals and system documentation:

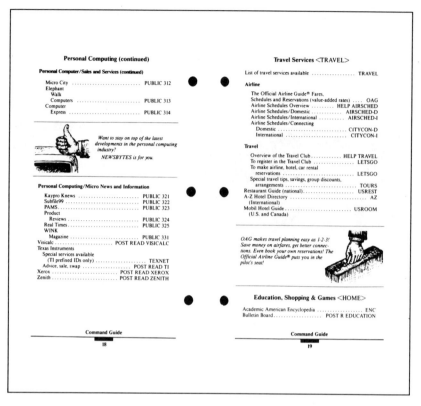

Figure 4.23. The Source command guide, typical pages.

Instructional Purpose

The user wants something to read before he signs on to the system for the first time, provided the seller is not offering formal instruction.

Reference Purpose

He wants something at the terminal to refer to when he encounters difficulty.

Descriptive Purpose

He wants something that describes the various kinds of information available within the service.

Visualization purpose

He wants something to illustrate the applications that he can make of search results.

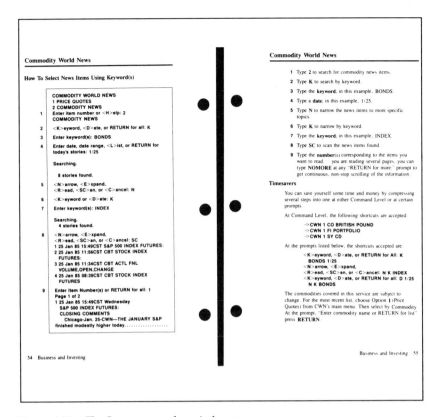

Figure 4.24. The Source manual, typical pages.

The seller wants a manual that underscores the ease of using the service, encourages use, satisfies the user, and answers questions. Too often the author of a manual tries to meet all of these four goals in one volume, and the result is a manual that is useful for none of these purposes. Often subsections of manuals are not prepared by the same part of the organization. In other situations they tend to be stitched together from small pieces prepared by many different authors, and some pieces are usually missed. As a result, the manual and the online helps, for example, are not coordinated, use different language to describe the same features, and end up thoroughly confusing the user. Customer service departments are often not coordinated with either the manual or the online help and thus, if the user calls the 800 number, he will get yet another explanation.

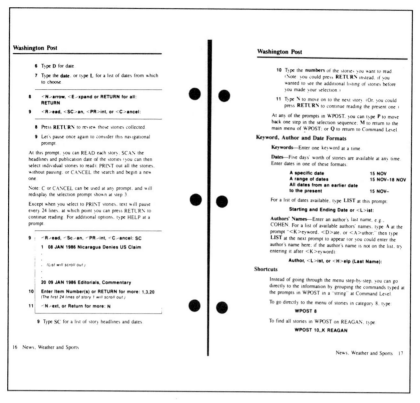

Figure 4.25. The Source manual, typical pages.

A MARKETING OPPORTUNITY

It seems contradictory that nearly every provider of an electronic information service publishes a "print-on-paper" manual when the business of such organizations is to manage information "electronically." The constant publication of updating materials, getting updates to users, and getting users to update their manuals has been an expensive management problem for the industry, a problem no one has been able to turn into a profitable opportunity. While Rolls Royce can sell its user manuals for $350 each, the users of top-of-the-line online services are not willing to pay for online sellers to do a first-class job with manuals. One innovative marketing solution is to design online manuals that can be down-loaded to disk, if desired, free of charge. The updating can then be done on the mainframe when required. The reference purpose can be solved by excellent online helps. No organization has yet done either successfully.

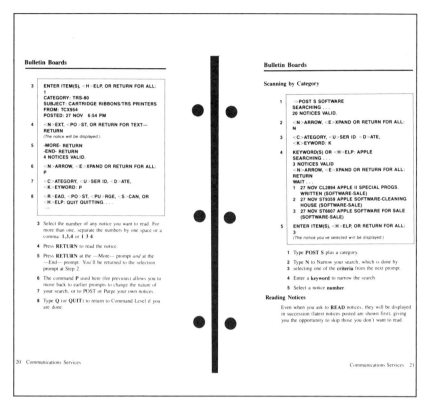

Figure 4.26.   The Source manual, typical pages.

Success Purpose: a Proposed New Mission for the Manual

The work of the manual should not be limited to the operational aspects of the system: there is too much novelty involved in online use and too big a gap in its integration into the rest of society to permit that level of complacency. At the bare minimum the manual could facilitate manageable searching and price risk and try to ensure some degree of search success before, during, and after the act of online searching.

An optimum manual would include searching and command technology in a guide to the larger process of communications (success purpose). This design would help the user cope more successfully with the changes online searching introduces into the user's environment and life. For example, a user may need to find the answer to a specific question. An optimum user's manual would contain several sections in support of overall communications activity sur-

THE ALL-IMPORTANT SECOND SALE   113

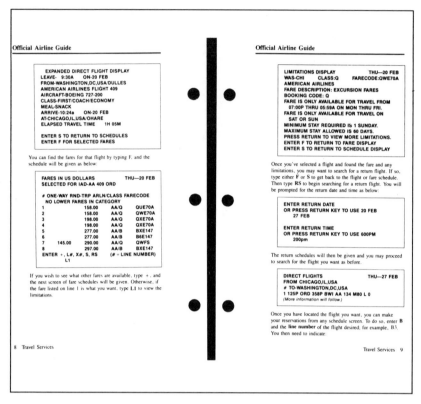

Figure 4.27.   The Source manual, typical pages.

rounding a single query: the operations/communications model might as shown in figure 4.28.

The first page would ask, What is the correct reporting format for this type of question and answer for your audience or for yourself? The manual would then discuss suggested report designs to prompt the user's creativity in finding and reporting an answer. Next it would consider posing questions in efficiently searchable terms that fit the chosen format. It would then offer command and search advice and, finally, show how to analyze typical search results to fit this chosen report format. Under this scheme the risk of search and reporting failure is managed to a much greater degree, and the chances of success with the enduser are multiplied. Greater success in the before-and-after communications planning and reporting translates into more desire to use the system.

The manual must fit into the world, too. To move beyond the technical is the basic challenge for marketing in questions involving (question type) → (best report formats for that type of question) → (best online searches for those types of questions and formats) → (usual kinds of findings) → (prototype report formats using this type of search findings)

Figure 4.28. User manual reporting sequence.

---

the user. Most manuals concentrate on the use of the system, naturally enough, but the system is part of the greater world, and the essence of success is how well it fits into the world of the user. McCarthy OnLine made this point in its advertising campaign, "Damned Unfair, Really" (see fig. 5.13). In the advertisement a user is shown having failed in his unstated assignment of using timely information properly for the ends of his company. The point is well taken because it does not matter how easy or difficult the search formulation might have been (or the degree of difficulty in the use of the manual, the documentation, the helps, the system, and so on); it is the idea that he either didn't proactively do the search or he didn't interpret the data in a proper report format (one that alerted him to its significance) that earned him the wrath of his boss. He has this problem because he has access to an online system (he couldn't have it if he didn't). Imagine a chapter on "How to win the praise of your boss by timely analysis and effective reporting of your proactive online search results"—it would be the most thumbed chapter in any user's manual.

TRANSPARENCY AND DENSITY IN THE MANUAL

The manual is a search and price risk management tool for the user and not, necessarily, just a road map to the use of the system. For every user there are several types of risk: financial; operational success/failure; social rejection by other users in SIGS and participative communication programs; boredom/excitement; and so on. The manual must initially assure (and keep reassuring) the user that the principal benefits of use are obtainable in a manner that makes his use of the command and operational technology of the system seem "transparent," compared to the "density" of the satisfactions he obtains through his participation and use. If the user is saddled with a reference, menu, and command system so interwoven and complex that it is continually frustrating, obscure, and obtrusive, the problem of coping with it will be what he will remember, probably with displeasure. From the marketing point of view the entire system should be idiot proof (transparent), and so should the manual and all of the system's documentation.

Notes

1. T. Levitt, *The Marketing Imagination* (New York: Free Press; 1983), 138.
2. *Office Information Systems in the Large Corporate Environment* (Manhasset: CMP Publications, 1986).

5
MAKING MARKETING
COMMUNICATIONS WORK

5.1. To Grow, the Online Industry Must Focus Its Marketing Communications on the Buyer, Ending the Seller's Preoccupation with His Systems and Their Features.

Examine the advertisements on television or in a newspaper or magazine. Since buyer-centered appeals are used in most advertising, you will notice that you have been judging a product-and-service beauty pageant as opposed to a quantitative competition based on merit. This beauty pageant is particularly benefit rich. Benefits are the topics of advertisement when products and services are technically similar to each other. Other than brand, benefits are often their sole distinguishing characteristics. In many ways a beauty pageant is a perfect showcase for this kind of selling because the competition plays to the one marketing strength of similar products. Products have even been designed to fit benefit formulas presumed to be winners in the pageant. A run-off on intrinsic technical merit might be disadvantageous to this type of product and very confusing for its buyers.

A beauty-pageant-inspired approach to benefits is finding increasing favor in high tech marketing, especially where large mixed markets such as those in the online industry have developed, and where products are technically similar, as in the electronics, computer, and telephone markets. It is proving useful because high tech products and services are conceptually obscure for many buyers and are therefore difficult (or impossible) for the buyer to compare on their technical merits. Coping with conceptual obscurity in high tech products has sparked several kinds of responses: in some buying organizations experts have been put on staff to manage the overall technical functions involved, for example, MIS managers, and marketers are changing their marketing and product design approach to accommodate a wider range of buyers, for example, Apple Computers.

Modern marketing has shown that qualitative comparisons are easier for the buyer and more productive for the seller, a lesson that is being painfully relearned in high tech. For simpler products like soap the established benefits (brand, health, cleanliness, enhanced attractiveness, etc.) may be the sum total of product knowledge for many consumers. A popular shaving foam has twenty ingredients, such as sodium metasilicate and coconut acid, listed on its spray can. It is a moderately complex industrial product, but it certainly isn't marketed as one. Almost no shaver knows what's in it or how the ingredients facilitate his shaving. Nor does he care, because it isn't sold comparatively on its technical merit but on its benefits—"medicated" and "protectant" (health), and "concentrated for closer and more comfortable shaves" (shaving comfort and attractiveness). How would the consumer decide the value of coconut acid, for example, to his shaving? For all the buyer knows every shaving foam may have the same ingredients or entirely different ones. As long as he is satisfied with his brand he will continue to buy the product on his normal purchasing schedule.

Like the purchaser of shaving cream, the purchaser of an online system is not interested in why the system runs fast (because it has a powerful mainframe computer). Nor is he interested in the fact that the online system is fast. His purchasing decision will be influenced only by his perception that online speed saves him time, just as the shaver is only interested in keeping his skin nice by "medicated" shaving. If shaving foam increases dramatically in price, however, the buyer may choose to switch brands more often or even permanently. In high tech purchases the calculation of price is usually more complicated than a few cents more for shaving cream. Amortization, switchover, service, and training costs enter the equation as additions to base price. These factors are not meaningful in the buying decision on shaving cream, so the habitual acquisition of the customary value-added benefits of the brand remains the deciding issue for the shaver.

Online services should be sold on their benefits, but not necessarily in a beauty pageant manner. For high tech products and services in the low to mid ranges of price, say, for example, yearly charges below the out-of-pocket cost of a good computer system, some of the same pricing factors affecting buyer behavior can be observed. When online charges tend to fall in this category, and online services have the high tech characteristic of being conceptually obscure to most buyers and users, this raises the strategic marketing issue of should they be sold more like computers (because they are high tech) or soaps (on their benefits)? As pointed out in chapter 2, pricing policy in the online industry directly influences all marketing choices. For the most part all types of buyers are mainly concerned with the benefits they get from ownership and use when pricing conditions permit. The two-step sales process requires a highly supportive system of marketing communications aimed at both the buyers' and users' needs and concerns. To summarize, marketing communications in the online industry will be more productive if they address benefits issues for two reasons: (1) to overcome the conceptual obscurity of high tech online systems by avoiding the issue in buyer communications (one isn't talking about obscure technology when one is talking about benefits), and (2) to take full advantage of the propensity of those buyers and users operating below the high price threshold to choose products and services by their benefits.

5.2. The Productivity of Marketing Communications Is Reduced When Technical Presentations Reduce the Size of the Effective Audience.

Features are favored in marketing communcations in the online industry. Explanations of the quantitative and technical features of a product or service can be difficult for the seller to present accurately and for the buyer to understand and remember. Yet they have a hard-to-resist psychological allure for the technically oriented seller even though a discussion of the technical features of a product or service is too narrow to have wide application as a stand-alone marketing message. Given the market advantage to be gained by stressing benefits, looking at why this happens can be useful to marketers in technically dominated organizations, like many of those in high tech or the online industry.

The effect of a technical presentation on the buyer is more like that of an invitation to contemplate the concepts and structure of the product or service itself, than an invitation to buy or use it. The seller's underlying assumption is that the buyer has the technical capacity and interest to trace for himself the invisible connections between the features and his needs. This is risky business below the high price threshold. The common practice of making connections evident to the buyer is ignored by trusting the buyer to correctly deduce the memorable and pleasing benefits of ownership and use. The buyer's motivation may be released and encouraged in some instances, but many responsible, well-educated buyers find technical materials demotivating, hard to understand, and tedious. The latter will be turned off and the former may not establish the right connections leading to sales and use.

In high tech the quantitative and the qualitative don't mix well in the same presentation. The reasons for this are found in the customs of expression and the use of logical information in scientific presentations. By definition technical and quantitative presentations, arrangements of facts, are not arguments or appeals; argument is forbidden: they must be quantitative, unambiguous, and unidimensional presentations. Consider some of the standard ways of presenting facts:

- in alphabetical order
- by order of magnitude
- from inside to outside
- from cause to effect
- in special topic sequences (e.g., in a list all of the electrical components followed by a list of all of the operator controls)

None of these are forms of active argument nor do they present benefits: they are passive partition and storage arrangements designed to aid accuracy during retrieval of data. Also, they must be detailed or they fail in their descriptive purpose. Sorting detail for significance can be distracting to sales. Attempts at translation from the technical are hopeless given the technical understanding of most marketers, sales people, buyers, and users.

Logically a technical presentation is not a good host for a memorable call to buy or a sizzling picture of the product or service in use. Their presence ruins the neighborhood, so to speak. (Said another way, the multidimensional, qualitative, value-added characteristics of a product or service cannot be visualized or mentioned easily because their very presence violates the rigor of technical presentation.) The tactical result is that they must be kept out, and their absence limits overall effect and appeal.

The functional allure of a technical description is strong for the seller. From the seller's point of view, reciting the features and specifications of the system or product are safe, low cost marketing communications. This precise calculation ignores the cost of miscommunications. It is true that

- factual presentations avoid exaggerated claims and emotive appeals
- specifications are constants that clearly apply in all situations where the product or system has to be presented, discussed, or used

- factual arrangements require no creativity to compile
- they are cheap to make and have the added bonus of a long shelf life
- the techniques of factual presentation are so familiar anyone can prepare them
- to the technically oriented, they are agreeable marketing materials that are easily approved by technically trained marketing and business executives because they fit the mindset

For these sensible reasons the drawbacks of technical materials as marketing communications—their limited audience appeal, their lack of persuasive and emotive content, etc.—are often overlooked or demoted to defects of secondary importance. For the sake of comfort marketing tactics can be ignored to the point where the technical approach converts into a de facto marketing plan.

The tactical point overlooked is that technical features are often peripheral to the buyer's purchase and use decisions below the high price threshold. If the technically oriented reader is conditioned through analysis to create a picture of the benefits of ownership and use for himself, the average reader is conditioned to believe that these connections will be made evident to him by the seller because of the importance of benefits in making buying decisions. For many, technical and quantitative analysis as part of a sale would be time consuming, cumbersome, and unwelcome.

An economic factor enters in as well: "Increased affluence and product differentiation enable the consumer to consider other factors as well as price when choosing goods. For the marketer the continuing problem of price management has become more complex, as decision making has to be related to other items in the marketing mix."[1] In large mixed markets many buyers of high tech products and services are incapable of successfully completing (from anyone's point of view) a real analysis. If it can't be done, reliance on technical features in marketing communications doesn't make any sense.

But a few key technical features are important in every online sale and must be included and addressed. "Will my microcomputer run your terminal emulation software?" is an example of the kind of question that might occur to any buyer. His questions must be answered directly, but the answers (yes or no) are peripheral to the technical reasons for software compatability. The full answer is complex and off the point of the question. Much more sophisticated questions about the detailed functions of online systems in an automated office or trading room would require and indeed merit lengthy and technically complex answers, and they would be to the point, but only because these are sales above the high price threshold. Whether they should be addressed in normal marketing communications is a tactical choice determined by whether their presence would add decisively to the motivation of the average buyer in the targeted market. If it wouldn't, they can be harmful distractions that can lead the buyer and seller into the obscure tangles of the kind always avoided in sales.

Are too many marketing communication factors and decisions in high tech affected by technophilia? Discovering the full range of qualitative, value-added characteristics of a high tech product or service is an outwardly turning creative task. So are the subsequent tasks of devising marketing communications and new products and services based on them. The seller must put himself in the buyer's shoes, because the benefits of an online service are hidden in the fertile minds and endless activities and applications of the buyers, users, endusers, and endconsumers of online information. Only they obtain and value the benefits. They have to be coaxed out of the users and buying organizations by the seller, which is a difficult, ambiguous social research project.

EMPATHY

Some of the important benefits of subscription and use are ephemeral, others are imprecise: all require some degree of humanistic interpretations. Fuzzy-sounding multidimensional data like these go against the grain of quantitatively oriented marketing managers and corporate executives. One result is resistance to its admission as marketing data. Part of this reaction is psychological dissonance with any datum that requires a creative "feel" to establish its full meaning. Both projective imagination and empathy must be used in making these decisions, and they are activities beyond the limit of comfortable behavior for many people. This kind of analysis is underdeveloped in the technically trained individual. When the two mind sets are united in one individual as they were in, say, generals George C. Marshall and J.F.C. Fuller, or in President Hoover and Lord Snow, the world benefits directly from their high order technical accomplishment linked to and expressed through their empathy. Their lives teach us that the true value of the technical is revealed in its relationship to the framework of human possibilities.

Benefits can be hard for the seller to identify and list, but they are easier for the average buyer to understand and remember. Knowledge of the buyer and the buying organization is critical when choosing key benefits from among the host of identified benefits. This seems to be true even when the benefits known to be valued highly are understood by the seller; they are still elusive and difficult to apply. In general, all benefits are easier to select and use in broad gauge communications like advertising, because a wide, self-selecting audience requires some generality in presentation. But on narrower occasions like the preparation of brochures, direct mail, or sales training programs for a campaign in a targeted market, it can be very difficult to choose among benefits because the fit should be tight to the audience selected. This can be unnerving when one's knowledge of the buyers and buying organizations is imperfect. It adds to the general dissonance over benefit issues. The tactical allure of the technical approach grows exponentially in these moments of hard choice.

The buyer can get by with knowing very little about the product beyond its benefits to him, but knowledge of both the benefits and the features is mandatory for the seller. That the key benefits can be positive influences in the decision-making processes of the buyer and user is a productivity advantage that may well offset the seller's discomfort with their ambiguous qualities. Knowledge of some or all the technical features may or may not be important to the hands-on buyer or user; in many cases it's optional. In the case of the removed initial buyer his interest and knowledge may stop with prices and benefits.

DISTINGUISHING BETWEEN BENEFITS AND FEATURES IN ONLINE SYSTEMS

A test for doing so is based on defining who gets what in the sale: the buyer gets all the benefits, and the seller keeps all the features. My critical review of marketing communications in the online industry in the United States and Great Britain indicates that marketers have not been discriminating successfully between features and benefits. The following definitions are proposed as aids to successful discrimination:

Benefits can only occur in the domain of the buyer and user. A benefit is obtained by purchase or use, that is, as a tangible mission achievement or psychological payoff, directly or indirectly resulting from the subscription to or use of an online system: it involves a quality, property, or characteristic of an online system that when understood, owned, or used results in a gain for the buyer. From this perspective the features of the system are *insignificant.* Examples of benefits are any quality or activity that earns or saves money; any social or professional interaction resulting from the presence or use of an online system that enhances self-esteem; any enhancements to personal, professional, organizational, or capital investment productivity; and so on.

Features are confined to the domain of the seller. A feature touches or influences the buyer or user but it never leaves the "possession" and "control" of the seller: it is an inherent quality, property, or mode of the social, economic, technical, or operational characteristics of the online system itself. Examples are baud rates, screen formats, the degree of user friendliness, the specific types of information in the databases and their range, protocols and search strategies, print products, accessibility, hours of operation, technical properties of all kinds, pricing and billing, operator manuals, user instructions, terminal emulation software, personnel, and so on.

The following is a list of general benefits to guide marketers when choosing between benefits and features. The benefits of most online systems can be expressed in these terms.

Ten general benefits of an online system

1. Saves time (staff expense)—because the searcher can review enormous amounts of data in seconds and on some systems can retrieve the full text of the search; thus retrieval is a one-step process.

2. Is more thorough—because searchers can choose to find the needle in the global haystack, they will conduct a search they would abandon if they had to do it manually. Searchers can review more timely pertinent data, including obscure sources that they would not or perhaps could not consult during a manual search. Searchers can approach the data from different angles of attack depending on the limitations of the system, their skill in searching, and their world view. Topics can be continuously monitored on some systems in many languages or in translation. All the available data can be consulted or reviewed if desired or if the cost/benefit exists.

3. Uses capital investment sparingly and holds staff expenses down—because the buyer neither invests in the acquisition, storage, management, and maintenance of print documents, computer tapes, fiches, and films, nor incurs operating expenses for trained staff to do archival and search tasks. Current research staffs are given cost-effective new tools by taking appropriate online subscriptions that enable them to be more productive, thereby eliminating the need for additional staff expense and capital investment.

4. Is glamourous, even talismatic—because its cachet—packaging, appearance, performance, scope, and technology—is global, modern, and high tech. The impressionable user can get a high-tech thrill. It is trendy in some knowledge, organizational, and business circles.

5. Is socially and professionally rewarding—because online searching allows users to discover, monitor, review, digest, deliver, choose among, weigh, and act on more data, thereby

earning them praise for their performance and recognition for their productivity, both of which lead to greater job satisfaction and professional growth.

6. Uses current investment in computer systems now—because the use of online systems immediately and directly increases the cost/benefit ratio of installed but underutilized systems.

7. Justifies the acquisition and use of new computer systems (a United States tax benefit)—because an online subscription is a solid professional justification for acquiring, installing, and using a new computer system.

8. Is current (up to the global information level in some databases)—the inherent delays in the production, translation, editing, printing, delivery, and integration of new data into periodicals and other traditional manual information systems, make electronic databases more topical than traditional sources all the way up to the global range of information. Its use can lead directly to more timely, valuable, and profitable investigations, decisions, and actions. Also, some timely information and data are quickly gathered just for and by online systems and filtered productively through their world view of economics, markets, market forces, politics, and domestic affairs around the world (a value-added service).

9. Allows convenience of time and place—because the modern equipped microcomputer is a portable system that can be used with almost any telephone, users may move around freely and still search effectively and professionally almost anytime they see fit.

10. Access enlarges the user's frame of reference (and increases his responsibility to be well informed)—because access to frequently updated wide-ranging (even global) electronic databases imposes an imperative to know what's going on. Access, not use, establishes an intelligence threshold, a standard of relevant awareness, against which one can be held accountable. Not knowing is now becoming unforgivable, self-defeating, even dangerous.

A REVIEW OF THE FREQUENCY WITH WHICH BENEFITS AND FEATURES APPEAR IN SOME UNITED STATES AND BRITISH VENDOR LITERATURE

As a way of testing the proposition put forward above on features and benefits, let's look at a few examples drawn from current customer literature and see if by using the ten benefits listed above as a test, features can be discriminated successfully from benefits. The examples also show the extent of the use of features in marketing communications. Below, benefits are marked B and features F.

Example 1: McCarthy Information Services (Financial Times). London.

"Before you make your next business decision . . . ask McCarthy, the international business information mastermind" [campaign theme]

The Features and Benefits of McCarthy:
High Quality Full Text Information [F]
Immediacy—Frequently Updated [B: benefit presented as a feature]
Instant Access [F]
International Accessibility [F]
Speed of Access [F]
Ease of Use [F]
Free Text Search Facility [F]
Retrieval Flexibility [F]
Monitoring Facility [F]
Headline; Context; Full Text Facilities [F]
Print Facility [F]
'Dump' Facility [F]
Controllable Costs [B: benefit presented as a benefit]
Archiving [F]
Hardware Independent [F]
Saving Searches [F]

McCarthy has used two benefits, "Immediacy—Frequently Updated" and "Controllable Costs" while mentioning sixteen features, 90 percent of the whole. The tactical result is to keep the bulk of the content in the domain of the seller.

Example 2: Pergamon Infoline, London.

Information Is Priceless. The Password Is Free. [campaign theme]

No one in business can put a price on good information—it is simply an essential part of the decision making process. But with so much information available in so many forms, it's hard to find exactly what you need. Whether you need to [know]:
. . . the latest company results of your competitors [B]
. . . credit ratings on your customers [B]
. . . potential new markets for your products [B]
. . . news items relating to your market [B]
Pergamon Infoline can help you! [F]
. . . accurate . . . up to date . . . world wide business news and interna-

tional corporate structures . . . through a telephone link in your office
[Benefit presented as a feature]
. . . free password . . . [F]
You simply pay for what you use. [F]

InfoLine has presented benefits 60 percent of the time.

Example 3: DIALOG (Lockeed Corp.), Palo Alto.

"To Finish in First Place" [campaign theme]

"DIALOG is the comprehensive information resource—a computer-based, online system giving you instant access to summaries of articles and reports, detailed financial data and directory listings on companies, statistics, full-text articles and newswires—from a pool of over 100 million items. [F] With information on virtually every subject in the world, DIALOG is the expert's and professional's first choice for information. [F]
DIALOG—The Online Service for the Professional [F]
Immediate Answers [B]
Pay Only for What You Use [F]
Available When You Need It [B]
The DIALOG Experts [F]
See DIALOG in Action [F]

DIALOG has presented benefits in 30 percent of the instances cited.

Example 4: IMNET (International Marketnet—Merrill Lynch and IBM), New York

"The IMNET Story" [campaign theme]

. . . IMNET has emerged with a well timed response . . . information and communication systems to implement those new [financial] strategies. [B]
The IMNET system uses advanced communications. . . . and an IBM-based architecture . . . [F]
. . . [firms] can also preserve their current investments in data processing resources. [B]
. . . a system that can change and grow with the firm's requirements. [F: this feature hides a cost benefit]
. . . an organization of people with uncommon skills. [F]

IMNET has presented benefits in 40 percent of its presentation.

Example 5: Kyodo News International (Dow Jones News/Retrieval), Tokyo.

"JAPAN ECONOMIC DAILY MEETS AMERICA'S DEMANDS" [campaign theme]

Japan Economic Daily is the broadest, most informative timely Japanese Financial data source available . . . [F]
Japan Economic Daily is electronically published by Kyodo News International . . . Japan's largest international new agency. Working with over 1,500 Kyodo news correspondents, *Japan Economic Daily* brings—TOMORROW'S NEWS—ON-LINE TODAY! [F]
Go to the primary source [F]
Kyodo [F]
Your Access Code to Japan [F]
Consider These News Applications [F]
Be on top of current market opening measures. . . [B]
Follow joint venture news . . . [F: this feature hides a benefit]
Trace yen/dollar fluctuations . . . [F]
Watch . . . the economy . . . [F]
Discern . . . political movements . . . [F]
Read first-hand [Governmental] reports . . . [F]
Follow Japan's role in . . . Pacific Basin countries . . . [F]

Kyodo has presented benefits in 7 percent of its presentation.

Comparison of the use of features and benefits in these presentations shows agreement with the very strong trend toward citing the technical features of online services to the exclusion of dominant presentations of buyer and user benefits. The pattern shown in figure 5.1 is typical of the industry as a whole.

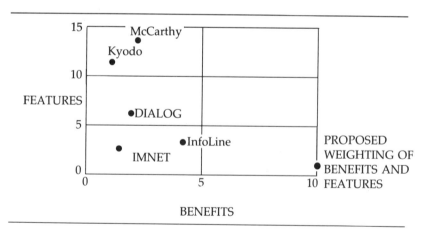

Figure 5.1. Comparison of the frequency of the use of features and benefits in some typical marketing brochures.

A PROPOSED GUIDELINE FOR THE RATIO OF FEATURES TO BENEFITS IN MARKETING COMMUNICATIONS

Marketing communications are made to persuade, stimulate, and release the motivation of the buyer to acquire and use the seller's products and services. They must tackle the buyer's motivations and his domain of concern and control. The graph depicts the extent of feature/benefit imbalance in the examples cited which are, by the way, simply typical representatives of the overall industry approach to the use of features and benefits in marketing communications. Too few value-added characteristics (those found only in the buyer's domain of interest) are addressed in the examples above. The emphasis in these examples results in exposing the domain of the seller at the expense of the buyer's concerns.

The full application of benefits to the marketing communications of most online organizations would amount to a de facto repositioning of the company, products, and services in the market. A ratio of two features to ten benefits is recommended as a guideline for marketers to assure that marketing communications are heavily weighted to the domain of the buyer. (One marketing manager reported that on any given testing occasion her sales force couldn't name more than one benefit in each six tries, despite its intensive training and drill on the specific benefits of the online system.)

5.3. Review of the Current Use of Ideas and Images to Show Benefits in the Online Industry

Visual literacy is on the rise around the world, and effective marketing communications use pictures as persuasively as they use words. Up to this point our discussion of benefits has been confined to language presentations, but images are also widely used to express benefit messages, and we will now examine some of the details of that process. Everything the company presents to the customer, from the physical design of tangible products like a computer console down to the typography of a rate card, has gained in marketing importance through the successful contributions of graphic and industrial design.

The visual qualities of product designs and marketing communications are as consciously managed in high tech marketing as any other marketing factor; consider, for example, the hugely successful design programs at Apple and IBM. In small and large companies technology, product, packaging, graphics, and ergonomics, are all included in a strategic marketing approach that states the seller's commitment to the market and the product. That product design has become a major selling point for high tech products and services reflects the fact that the educated buyer in all nations is becoming more cultivated, visually literate, and critically aware. Apple, IBM, and others find their designs praised to the skies, and this genuine admiration (and pride of ownership) plays an important part in the marketing image and success of the company.

Note: the definitions used for the analysis of marketing communications examples are:

Explicit copy. The reality and experience that we describe in marketing communications by means of words and pictures, usually the marketing message to the buyer audience.

Implicit content. The meanings that arise from the combinations of words, shapes, sizes, physical arrangement, styles, colors, and technical details of marketing communications.

Audiences. Those who produce the advertisement, those who are the market targets of the communications producers, and all of those who may be addressed indirectly or who comprehend the communication.

INTRODUCTION TO THE TELETRADE CAMPAIGN   Teletrade's City Business System (CBS) repositions the traditional telephone market by the introduction of an automated telecommunications product, a microprocessor-driven telephone/telex and order/data management console for currency and commodity traders. In the advertisement that introduced it to the market (not shown here) the copy stressed that traders may have only seconds to close the loop on a deal, and that the new Teletrade system permitted "instant" world wide communication just by touching the right sector on the touch-controlled screen. Other features of the CBS system were mentioned in the copy but the benefits of touch control dominated the advertisement.

EXPLICIT COPY   In figure 5.2 the system is presented as a successful trading support system currently used in twenty two countries. Only features of the system are mentioned in the advertisement, particularly the different types of screen faces available. Benefits are not mentioned in the copy nor are they shown in the photographs. The key benefit of the CBS system—replacement of the traditional telephone handset and system—is neither mentioned nor directly demonstrated.

The City Business System from British Telecom Teletrade has very quickly become standard equipment for many banks and financial institutions around the world where fast and effective communications are essential.

The CBS is not only a fully comprehensive and very modern phone system, providing anything up to 1024 lines, it is also capable of storing and displaying thousands of pages of data that can be accessed simply using a VDU touchscreen.

Already well established in over 150 companies in 22 countries, the CBS is proving to be the dealers choice for very good reasons – primarily because of the system's ability to be tailored exactly to the customer's communications needs, and because the CBS is built with the future in mind, users are confident that their system will always be right up to date.

For example, today's CBS offers enhancements such as:
- full colour monitors to help clarify the function of each key;
- slim and totally flicker-free 'plasma screens';
- 'turbo units' allowing faster handling of messages through an existing system;
- line display modules which let controllers see at a glance the status on up to 160 lines;
- the CBS Call Management which provides an output to an optional call logger.

And, with world networks of CBS terminals, more and more companies are making the concept of 24-hour world trading a reality.

more Cities more Business more Systems

The City Business System in action in the dealing room of the London branch of Chase Manhattan Bank NA

COLOUR MONITORS

PLASMA SCREENS

For further information on CBS or any other British Telecom communications products and systems, call Teletrade today on +44 272 217050. UK 0272 217050 (available 24 hours). Or telex 449217 BT TAN G

Alternatively write to British Telecom Teletrade, Marketing Dept. Garrard House, 31-45 Gresham Street, LONDON EC2V 7DN

British Telecom
Teletrade

The overseas equipment marketing unit of British Telecom

Figure 5.2. An advertisement by Teletrade that draws together many of the themes discussed in Section 5.3. Reprinted by kind permission of British Telecom.

IMPLICIT COPY (LEVEL ONE IMPRESSIONS)   The clever headlines fail to create an easy-to-understand context for the photographs and copy because what they assert is not particular to the CBS system. The dominant photograph is documentary in style and not evocative of the excitement and energy of a trading room. The CBS console is shown near the center of the larger photograph surrounded by the screen faces of other systems. The image is hemmed in on three sides. All visual elements balance. This is unfortunate because the effect is too static to show the dynamic qualities of the benefit, and the small sizes of the photographic images hide detail.

IMPLICIT COPY (LEVEL TWO IMPRESSIONS)   Another aspect of this advertisement that may strike the reader's eye disconcertingly and disadvantageously in terms of the message is the industrial design of the console, a strategic marketing issue in and of itself. It arises when the industrial design of the Teletrade console is examined closely: the screen graphics and plastic casing of the CBS system look strikingly out-of-date. Their appearance raises a question about Teletrade's commitment to the *technology* and not, as one might initially suppose, a question about Teletrade's commitment to industrial design. This doubt, in turn, suggests that Teletrade is not committed to this product or to this market.

Industrial design is an international corporate art form that builds into the product strategic messages about technology, the product, the company, and its society. When new products are rolled out, their "design statements" are read as carefully as any other marketing "copy." All the marketing messages generated by the design and styling of the product itself must agree with all of the other marketing communications about the product. In the case of the CBS system, agreement is missing; the console design can be read to mean, perhaps, that the Teletrade project is a catch-up effort based on retrofitting older terminals and not a major new product as claimed.

AUDIENCES.   The removed buyer and the top-of-the-line trader/user are the main audiences for the advertisement. The design of the CBS system suggests that cyberphobia is not a major issue in this market, or that if it is, benefits so far outweigh fears that the system is acceptable to traders.

EXPLICIT CONTENT.   Lotus Signal and Lotus Software (1-2-3 or Symphony versions) are the two products advertised. Signal gets top billing by a ratio of 15 to 1. The copy is breezy and energetic and fits perfectly with the image of the screen bursting through the page. It makes strong points in an aggressive and forceful context. The key appeal is to current Lotus users with financial responsibilities (there are several million copies of Lotus 1-2-3 in use in the United States and Great Britain) who are urged to integrate their electronic spread sheet software (1-2-3 and Symphony) with Signal, making the user more competitive and productive. The two products form a third tool—a new electronic online financial spread sheet. The third tool is shown on the screen face. The well-established brand image of Lotus 1-2-3 lends its credibility to Signal by being technically compatible. This design produces a powerful new benefit, and new value is added to both tools. Also, most significantly, existing software and training investments are enhanced by the addition of Signal.

IMPLICIT COPY. Traditional printed stock quotations are shown literally being destroyed by Signal's urgent power. Signal is shown to be abruptly changing the financial information market. The headline and the screen face bursting through the newspaper page give an impression of power. The newspaper advertisement is printed in black and white in half-page format. The type is well laid out in three short columns for easy reading. The dynamic context of the screen and headline dominates all other meanings.

AUDIENCE. The audience is composed of the current and potential users of 1-2-3 and Symphony, supposedly a high tech lot if there ever was one. The model of the user is rather surprisingly, then, treated as one with some cyberphobia but not enough to be deterred by any new complications introduced by Signal. The appeal is to the reader who wants to be even more competitive than he or she now is; the benefit is the intellectual support to do so.

COMPARISON OF THE LOTUS AND TELETRADE ADVERTISEMENTS (SEE FIGURE 5.2.) Lotus uses strong visual means to make its advertisement dynamic. When it appeared in the newspaper, the screen face seemed literally to burst through the page. The illusion heightened the message and suited the marketing needs very well. It held the reader's interest because it made the point of how static a newspaper really is. Teletrade has developed a static format and undynamic look that dampens the claim it makes for the speed and effectiveness of CBS system. The reasons are related to the balanced visual aspects of the layout and the look of the advertisement; overall, the advertisement is not a strong argument for the benefits of the product. Both advertisements are positioned to do the same job in similar markets, each feature the screen of the product and they are different as day is from night.

LIVE FRO

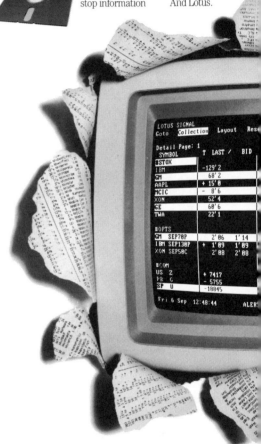

...AND COMING SOON TO PHOENIX.

It's like being there, right on the Exchange floor. Signal™ from Lotus.® It's the real time market quote system that offers you up-to-the-second quotes, plus instant personal computer analysis capabilities at a cost-effective price.

LOTUS
INTRODUCES
SIGNAL

No modems, no delays, just non-stop information

that you can easily use and technical analysis because Signal uses FM telephone charges.

One thing more. Alo and support of the wor Lotus. Signal. And Lotus.

Figure 5.3.   An advertisement by Lotus. © Lotus Development Corporation.

WALL ST.

te portfolio valuation r Symphony." And there are no access or

al you get the service supplier of software. from Wall St.

ATTEND A SIGNAL SEMINAR—FREE
To find out more about the benefits of Signal, attend one of the free seminars below by calling, toll free, 1-800-882-4432, ext. 501.

DATE	LOCATION
• October 14	Phoenix Hilton
• October 15	Arizona Biltmore (Scottsdale)
• October 16	Hilton Pavilion (Mesa)

Lotus Signal

COMPARISON OF THE LOTUS AND THE SECOND PHINET ADVERTISEMENT, "THE ULTIMATE BUSINESS CONNECTION" (SEE FIGURE 3.6). Both advertisements work at selling two products simultaneously. The PHINet advertisement lacks message dominance and may respond too conservatively to a model of a customer thought to be highly cyberphobic. Conversely, the Lotus advertisement expresses product and benefit dominance in an atmosphere of more cyberphobia than I would have ever predicted for 1-2-3 users. PHINet's advertisement demonstrates the drawback of hedging one's bets: Lotus's shows the utility of boldness in pushing one product forward to emphasize the benefits.

5.4. It May Be Very Difficult for the Buyer Proactively to Appreciate, Understand, or Match the Features of High Tech Online Services or Products to the Benefits He Desires or to Those Needed by the Buying Organization

High tech myths like the "paperless office" or the performance promises made for nonexistent "vaporware" and other examples of promotional hype have been damaging to buyer enthusiasm, motivation, and confidence in high tech markets. The reader will recall Lynn M. Salerno's ominous conclusion: "The over enthusiastic vendors and other boosters of automation and the computer age are hoist with their own petard."[2] The failure of a match between the available benefits and the buyer's vision of his information and research needs is a needs-gap. Needs-gap analysis studies the mind-set and perceptions of the buyer and his view of his options; it then uses these findings for guidance in the development, marketing, and management of products and services. Unlike the needs-gaps caused by the endless technical bugs and mysteries that disturb buyer perceptions in computer and software deals, the needs-gaps in the online industry are mainly caused by fuzzy buyer perceptions of the benefits of automated information—essentially a marketing and marketing communications issue under the right circumstances. Below the high price threshold, gaps are created and prolonged by feature-oriented marketing communications, complex pricing strategies, erratic database acquisitions, and technical aspects of knowledge product construction and market positioning. The gap is heavily colored by high tech's problems as a whole.

According to Davidow[3] and other high tech marketers, up-to-date high tech marketing programs can be profitably driven by what could be called a "gap-recognition program" designed to

- reverse and inform the attitudes of the buyer and the market
- repair the weakness of the seller in making, positioning, delivering, and servicing products and services that are not attuned to buyer perceptions and market needs
- build the image of the seller as a solid and effective company

Formal assessment of the extent of the gap can be done in a number of different ways. Choosing a method will depend on market, pricing, marketing style, resources, need, and commitment. Piecing together the spotty evidence about gap assessments suggests that the following general, five-step outline sums up one way that a needs-gap program could be undertaken.

(1) Survey the buyers in a specific market to estimate the degree of satisfaction that initial buyers have with their current information options (online database services may or may not be included). Current communication and research investments, activities, and processes of the buyer and the buying organization would be explored as fully as possible.

(2) The online vendor's sales force and marketing team, working with experts knowledgeable in the market, independently estimate the market's needs. (This is an optional step if the product or marketing manager is from the industry being studied.)

(3) The survey and the estimate are compared. The company can then identify the real strengths and the perceived weaknesses of the service. Marketing decisions can be made at this point.

(4) Where necessary, a second survey, based on the findings (see step 3) can be undertaken to gauge the perceptions of the buyer's view of any online service's ability to satisfy his needs. (This step is optional if the product is market dominant, well respected, technically perfect, and leading its competition on all counts. If the product manager has studied the market closely over time and if major enhancements are not being planned for introduction in the near future, the need for this step is also diminished.)

(5) The study would find the specific benefits the buyer wants but doesn't think can be obtained from the online service (or anywhere) at this time. If the benefits are available or can be provided, a needs-gap has been identified and measured.

At least three types of strategic marketing actions can emerge from the intelligence gained about needs-gaps (depending, of course, on market, products and services, pricing, marketing style, and resources).

(1) Where the gap is found to be small those specific items that are isolated and defined can be named product, operational, and communication improvement targets.

(2) Where the gap is large (but reasonably manageable) targets for new or increased marketing efforts can be selected, product development can be undertaken, and even some repositioning of products may be warranted and cost justified, because the problem is still confined to the buyer's perceptions of the service and its products in terms of his expectations.

(3) If a very large gap is confirmed—it will come as no surprise, of course—its exact nature could trigger a process of major product development.

The technical stability of online systems helps their image in the high tech market. Yet it should not be overlooked that online systems are relatively dynamic, technology-based, and open-ended operations. Under normal market conditions there is always a gap between the current subscriber's image and understanding of the service, and the actual service. It is safe to assume that there is always a gap on pricing. Needs-gap analysis teaches that marketing may choose to deal with all buyer and buying occasions as separate marketing issues that deserve tailored communication sales programs. This is a sound practice because each class of buyers has differing impressions of the utility and value measures of the service.

Reduction in the sizes of needs-gap magnitudes is one of the true measures of the success of marketing efforts. In effect, two strategies are used. First, the benefits marketed must be addressed specifically to closing the gap for that class of buyer and buying organization. Second, the products must be repositioned if the gap remains wide and the penetration rate is unsatisfactory. In the first instance, marketing the appropriate benefits usually does not require a major overhaul of marketing communications programs because the positioning is correct, and the major campaign themes are correct. Either the right benefits need to be stressed more and highlighted from among a series of benefits, or, as is more often the case in the online industry, emphasis in marketing communications needs to change from features to benefits. Repositioning is the expensive choice. In a high tech market dominated by another firm, it gets very expensive. Therefore, repositioning cannot be undertaken lightly.

Few online markets allow defensible businesses. Database development is too simple and inexpensive for anyone to feel secure.

Customers are very cost and service conscious, and can be wooed away. The best defense available may be a gut level commitment to a market the service can hope to dominate eventually. Defense requires that everyone—where possible—has to be signed on for the long term. It also means that opportunities in other online markets might have to be passed up because the commitment to winning and keeping a valuable market is a major resource limit, as well as a great opportunity. Unity of strategic purpose, quality in products and services, and overall consistency of execution are demanding and expensive masters. Executing the business and marketing plan perfectly may not be enough, as market dominance in the industry increasingly becomes a high stakes business.

5.5. Positioning Issues

A brilliant technology isn't enough to assure product success in the high tech market. Great technologies are going begging. A product has to be shaped to fit its market while it's being conceived and designed. To do that successfully its configuration and characteristics must be matched to the needs and perceptions of the targeted market. Because of this requirement every product has a position in the market based on the quality of its fit; the issue for marketing, then, is to assure that the position is the one it has chosen. Marketing's role is to create, manage, and dominate a favorable position by helping design products and services, and creating the human, online, and printed communications embodying the products, the company, and the industry to the buyer.

POSITIONING DEFINED IN OVERSIMPLIFIED TERMS

Ries and Trout define positioning as a set of strategic communication activities that marketers must engage in in their chosen market, with special awareness of those factors that limit their ability to communicate productively. The goal is to make a product or service fit the market so well that the marketing communications needed to support the program are simple, direct, and powerful enough to make a lasting impression on the buyer. They say that "positioning is not what you do to a product. Positioning is what you do to the mind of the prospect. That is, you position the product in the mind of the prospect."[4]

In the early 1980's Regis McKenna expanded positioning by factoring the competition into the positioning equation during his marketing consulting in Silicon Valley. "Positioning is the psychological location in the consumer's mind, pertaining to the relative qualities a company, product, or service may have with respect to its competition."[5] A decade of experience in the high tech market had shown that the mind-set of the customer included parallel and significant references to the competition.

William Davidow, former senior vice president of sales and marketing for Intel Corporation, adds to the definition of positioning in the late 1980's: "The positioning of a technology product is not merely a fabrication of the advertisement agency and the marketing department. Rather, a position is the outgrowth of the market being served. It must be designed into the product [by marketing]. The product must exemplify the company's philosophical beliefs about itself and its products."[6] In simplified terms, the casual relationship between the customer and product positioning is now defined as follows:

Market/buyer→Company→Competition→Product positioning
Market/buyer acceptance and product performance→Company→ Refined position

Experience has modified the approach to positioning in high tech marketing: a high tech product is conceived, produced, and sold contextually in the industry environment against which it will be measured by the buyer; it conveys values to the buyer; it reflects back to the buyer his own needs and concerns by having buyer-centered characteristics that are built into the product using marketing's market and buyer knowledge.

SPECIAL ASPECTS OF POSITIONING IN HIGH TECH

Marketing's ability to gather and interpret market intelligence from the buyer and user plays a big role in a high tech product's acceptability and sales. Those who are aware of them at all probably think of online services as a high technology phenomenon, a little part of the telecommunications and computer revolutions. For marketers that means recognizing that buyers of online services see themselves as subject to the forces at work in the negatively charged high tech market. It follows, then, that in positioning products and services in the online industry negative market factors have to be taken into account. (Keep in mind that most prospects for online services are presented with two buying decisions in a negative attitudinal environment.) Positioning the system and products as benefit-rich and rewarding is important to overall success. Marketing must also play a major role in creating and building the online products themselves and the communications that keep the user coming back to the terminal. The central issue is always the customer's relationship to, use of, and involvement with the service and its benefits. It is in this sense that a clear positioning opportunity can be observed between the first and second sales. The first sale is more removed and rational than the second sale; the second sale is closer in and more emotional because the service is an actual and dynamic part of the user's life. Marketing and support services must understand and use the emotional aspect of online services use as part of positioning.

5.6. Outline for Improved Marketing Communications

- When the needs-gap is small, better marketing communications, usually telling the benefits, can help close it; when the gap is larger, repositioning strategies can close it. Some gaps can't be closed by marketing tactics; product redesign is then called for.
- Increase your understanding of the buyer's motivation, mindset, activities, and interests. Express your understanding as benefits addressed to the first and second sales separately.
- Be correctly positioned in terms of the market and the buyer's needs. Find the needs-gaps, target them, and position accordingly.
- Use messages that reach the buyer. Make sure that marketing communications are biased in favor of the buyer's domain. Keep in mind the effects of the high tech environment on attitudes.
- Set realistic goals for marketing communications programs. An example of such a goal might be: a 15 percent increase in the awareness of all London-based Eurobond traders of the three key benefits of the online system within the next ninety days at a cost of £2,500 in creative, production, and direct mail expenses.
- Rise to the creative challenge by setting the highest goals consistent with your market in the conception, analysis, and design of the system, the products, and the marketing campaign.

5.7. Marketing Communication Examples

As pointed out above, needs gaps can be addressed and dealt with by marketing communications; in fact, this is one of the best ways of efficiently closing the gap. The following examples will offer occasions where the nature of the needs-gap of the seller's service is apparent. Positioning will be examined as well; the attempts at repositioning are of special significance to us at this point. The examples demonstrate in some important way the themes discussed in this chapter. All of the examples are drawn from advertising campaigns because advertising is one of the best, if not *the* best, tool available for reaching the secondary and tertiary markets of the online industry. Print advertising is very well suited to small budgets and can easily handle the complexity of the messages required in the online industry.

 Note: The definitions used for the analysis of marketing communications variables are:

Explicit copy: the reality and experience that we use words and pictures to describe in marketing communications, usually the marketing message to the buyer audience.

Implicit content: the meanings that arise from the combinations of words, shapes, sizes, physical arrangement, styles, colors, and technical details of advertisements.

Audiences: those who produce the advertisement, those who are the market targets of the advertisement's producers, and all of those who may be addressed indirectly or who comprehend the advertisement.

5.8. Leadership Positioning Strategies

EXPLICIT COPY Lexis claims to be the best computer-assisted legal research service—the front runner. The claim influences the reader's perception of the service's leadership position in the industry. The advertisement uses visual and verbal puns drawn from the legal field to keep things light. The copy is presented as "evidence."

IMPLICIT COPY The headline and claims overwhelm a cartooned attorney, who is knocked flat by the "evidence." The copy block is designed to be skimmed by the reader, who, after skimming, would retain an impression of superiority. The lightness in tone is achieved by cleverly counterpointing the copy and the illustration.

AUDIENCES The audience is the hands-on initial buyer of computer-aided legal research services who owns or operates his own PC system.

 Mead's advertisement drew a sharp response from the competition in the legal market, demonstrating the importance assigned

LEXIS.
THE EVIDENCE IS
OVERWHELMING.

 When it comes to computer-assisted legal research, there's no contest. LEXIS® is the leader. Over 150,000 legal professionals now use LEXIS—40,000 times a day. Read why.

LEXIS is the largest. It's the most comprehensive, on-line, full-text database of law and legal information in the world. And *continuously* updated.

LEXIS is the fastest. 90 percent of all searches are completed on average in 15-20 seconds.

LEXIS is the most available. We're open 23 hours a day—15 hours on weekends.

LEXIS is the most reliable. It's the only legal search system with its own telecommunications network—MeadNet®.

LEXIS is cost-efficient. The speed and full-text retrieval of LEXIS, plus off-peak discounts, *plus* off-line printing, make LEXIS more economical to use than any other service.

LEXIS gives you more law—not less law. Only LEXIS gives you slip opinions. Shepard's®. Access to unpublished opinions. Auto-Cite®.

LEXIS gives you NEXIS®—the largest on-line, full-text database of news and information in the world. Millions of stories, articles and reports that don't turn up in law libraries —all instantly accessible to you.

LEXIS service sweeps the field. We have offices in 20 states, the District of Columbia—and 31 cities. Plus continuous, personal follow-up and on-going instruction.

LEXIS usage up nearly 20% in one year. And the number of new LEXIS accounts rose significantly in 1983. Every day more judges, lawyers, corporations, federal agencies, state and local governments, law firms, law schools in 50 states and foreign entities use LEXIS more than all other services.

Find out why getting more out of LEXIS could be one of the smartest decisions you've ever made. Write Jack W. Simpson, President, Mead Data Central, Dept. TRI3, P.O.1830, Dayton, OH 45401. Or call us toll-free at **1-800-227-4908.**

LEXIS NEXIS
Who. What. Where. When. _Now._

Figure 5.4.   An advertisement by Mead Data Central. © Mead Data Central, Inc.

to leadership positioning in a competitive industry segment. Here is Westlaw's "instant replay" of Mead's advertisement.

EXPLICIT COPY   The new content is a counterclaim. Westlaw's content functions like countertestimony in a court of law or like an attorney's summation of a case to a jury—they got into the spirit of

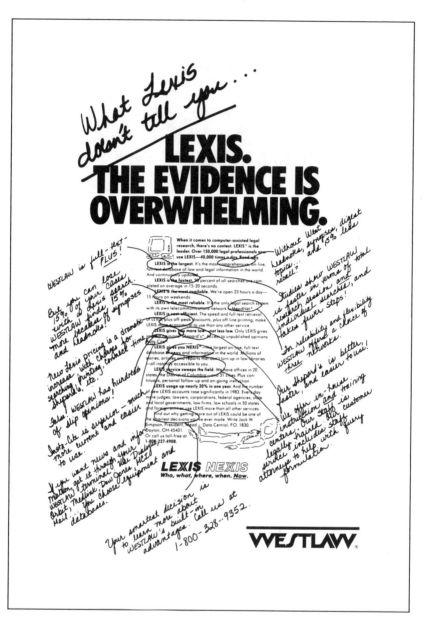

Figure 5.5. An advertisement by West Publishing Company. © 1984, "What Lexis Didn't Tell You." *Reprinted with permission of West Publishing Co., St. Paul, Minn.*

the first advertisement. Point after point is capped and expanded. The total effect is, at first glance, a bold graphic discrediting of Mead's claims.

IMPLICIT COPY   Westlaw's additions produce a densely packed type field. The Lexis original displayed 100 words of copy to its readers by the time they reached the fifth of its ten paragraphs of claims, and Westlaw has added about 75 more words in the same space—roughly one third of the whole Lexis advertisement. Nearly 700 words are jammed into one page. Clearly, no one is meant to read all of the claims and counterclaims. It is the impression of numerous substantial counterclaims that counts.

This advertisement demonstrates the power of context to establish meaning in advertising. A very expressive element is the cartooned attorney, figure 5.6. Westlaw has succeeded in changing the reading of his expression from one of being "overwhelmed by Lexis' evidence" to one of "being uncertain about Lexis." The inversion is caused by the placement of written commentary in close proximity to his head; it refocuses the meaning the reader assigns to his expression. This one example demonstrates how Westlaw creates a new context for interpretation of all of the advertisement's elements, overriding and to some extent voiding the original context.

AUDIENCE   The same audience as before, preferably those who had read Mead's original advertisement.

Figure 5.6.   The expressive attorney. © 1984, "What Lexis Didn't Tell You." *Reprinted with permission of West Publishing Company.*

SUMMARY AND COMPARISON OF THESE TWO VERSIONS
OF THE SAME ADVERTISEMENT. What needs-gap of the lawyer is addressed if he deals with the number one online service?
Quantity? Is not the law just that, the law? Each system would deliver
that to him, surely. Westlaw used to be cheaper than Lexis, but there
is no strong appeal to cost/benefit or price. The issue is positioning
Westlaw as the leading legal service. Leading lawyers must want to
deal with the industry leader.

Did either company achieve its positioning choice? Mead is
revealed (in the Westlaw version) to have been too partial to its own
case when it presented its "evidence." Westlaw nails Mead in sins
of omission, and then promptly does the same thing itself. Westlaw's
extensive rewrite omits addressing by counterclaim Mead's key positioning argument, its 150,000 users. Unless Westlaw can bat it down,
Mead's claim must stand as "admissible evidence" under Westlaw's
own rules of evidence procedure.

Those who enjoy watching a good brawl may well find Westlaw's version entertaining and persuasive. Those who prefer gentle-
manly debate might find the tone uncomfortable. Anyone looking at
the facts in the advertisements may find that neither case is made
completely satisfactorily. Mead could have used a presentation of
comparative advantages demonstrating, if they could, that the evidence is on their side, but admitting that the other guy has something
going for him too. That approach would have left little ground for
Westlaw to attack. Liveliness in advertisements attracts readers, but
Westlaw could have used a dispassionate argument of comparative
disadvantages, a tack that might have been more persuasive to a wider
group of readers. It is likely, but by no means certain, that an advertisement of this latter type would have been dull when compared
to the current version; and if dull, it is certain that it would have had
to be published many times to get the full message across.

In somewhat the same vein, here is a Shark/Wang advertisement that addresses the positioning problem from starboard rather
than port.

EXPLICIT COPY The appeal used in this advertisement reaches
far beyond benefit claims for an online system to establish the idea
that all of the trading and back office functions in a financial house
are one integrated system with online included as just one of the
major communications elements. This is a needs-gap recognition of
a major problem. The total systems approach is a repositioning of the
real-time quotes market. Wang uses antithesis between the concepts
of passivity and menace as a positioning device for the online service.
In the "world" of this advertisement, Shark has been merely dangerous to Quotron's position up to now, but with Wang's technolog-

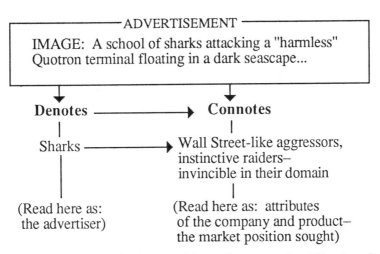

```
┌─────────────────ADVERTISEMENT─────────────────┐
│ IMAGE:  A school of sharks attacking a "harmless" │
│ Quotron terminal floating in a dark seascape...   │
│                                                 │
```

Denotes ──────────▶ **Connotes**

Sharks ──────────▶ Wall Street-like aggressors,
                                   instinctive raiders–
                                   invincible in their domain

(Read here as: (Read here as: attributes
the advertiser)   of the company and product–
                             the market position sought)

This approach is limited to specific audiences and publications because awareness of Shark's positioning depends on the reader's specific knowledge of the financial world, without which connotation is not possible

Figure 5.7.   Overlapped messages in an advertisement by Shark/Wang.

ical, marketing and financial power behind them they declare that are now deadly to Quotron. The advertisement targets one of the most difficult and solution-resistant problems in the financial market and the high-tech office environment, namely, making real-time systems coherent.

IMPLICIT COPY   Let's examine the uses of "shark" in this advertisement. The words and the visual images for shark refer the reader to the fish's appetite. The headline borrows language from a recent series of shark movies: "Just when Quotron thought it was safe to go back in the water." It creates a communications frame where Quotron appears timid and helpless, a victim. The image of Quotron is a cartooned screen console bobbing in the water while a school of sharks closes in for the kill (the reader knows this will end in a feeding frenzy). Behind the sharks, surfacing from the deep, is a dark force, Wang. All of this menace is shown converging on Quotron (and ADP and Telerate). The type and visual elements all support this theme, and the dark/bold character of the advertisement is dramatic.

AUDIENCES   The appeal is to those initial buyers who have endured the problems and costs of incompatible real-time systems. There are two levels of participants, initial buyers who use Quotron and Shark to provide their real-time market information, and new initial buyers at the company-wide level coping with the systems mess (CFO's?). The latter are bigger fish indeed, and the appeal of the advertisement is directed to them. The positioning design is to gain access to the market by filling the needs gap with an enriched mix, a turnkey approach to counter the positioning of firms like IMNET/ IBM and to take the market share of firms like Quotron by locking in the quote market with the computer sale. It remains to be seen if this will be a successful market method; it wasn't for IMNET, which recently went to a watery grave. The advertisement hinges on the credibility of Wang's extension into the financial market. Can Wang, a traditional power in office systems, follow Shark's wake into the financial deep waters? It remains to be seen.

COMPARISON OF SHARK/WANG AND WESTLAW'S RE-TREADED MEAD ADVERTISEMENT   Both of these advertisements depict a competing service in unflattering terms as part of an aggressive positioning plan. The advertisements are fundamentally similar despite their many superficial differences. Both rely on representational components to carry the load. Rigorous copy and representational techniques are avoided. Literal exposition gives way to expressive forms with stronger dramatic tension, thereby giving an impression of vitality (tension = energy = life). Westlaw's vigorous calligraphy and the angry gestures of the hand behind it produce the tension. In the Shark/Wang advertisement vitality is implied by the name "shark" and by the visual and verbal images and references to the deadly fish.

By departing from the norm of business to business advertising these advertisements automatically get our attention as anything out of the ordinary does. A novel representational approach, as demonstrated by Westlaw's advertisement particularly, creates an unexpected tension for the reader that exploits the representational context to the full.

There are other approaches to these issues. Here is one used by BusinessLand that explores some of the same country but from an entirely different point of departure. (As far as I can determine this was the first United States advertisement to use online services as a "technological leader" for selling other services. Shark/Wang came later.)

EXPLICIT COPY   BusinessLand focuses on a special needs-gap problem of the high tech office and uses online information systems

All we wanted was a system that would let us check with the whole world before making a split-second transaction.

C. Bruce Johnstone and Fred L. Henning, Senior Vice Presidents, Fidelity Investments

AZ: Phoenix, Scottsdale, Tempe. CA: Glendale, Huntington Beach, Irvine, La Jolla, Los Altos, Los Angeles, Manhattan Beach, Oakland, Orange, Puente Hills, Sacramento, San Diego, San Francisco, San Jose, San Mateo, Sherman Oaks, Sunnyvale, Walnut Creek. CO: Aurora, Denver. FL: Altamonte Springs, Coral Gables, Ft. Lauderdale, Tampa. GA: Atlanta, Smyrna. IL: Chicago. LA: New Orleans. MA: Boston, Framingham. MD: Rockville. MN: Minneapolis. MO: Clayton, St. Louis. NJ: Cherry Hill. NM: Albuquerque. NY: New York. OH: Cleveland. OR: Beaverton, Portland. PA: Philadelphia. TX: Austin, Dallas, Houston, Richardson, San Antonio. UT: Salt Lake City. VA: Rosslyn, Vienna. WA: Bellevue, Seattle. Call (800) 228-7463 for locations nationwide.

Figure 5.8.   An advertisement by Businessland.

almost as a pretext for the advertisement. This dramatic advertisement describes the sale of sixty PCs to Fidelity Investments, which uses them to access online systems, but the advertisement describes the national installation of the new PCs and their integration with Fidelity's existing online and computer systems in just ninety-six hours.

The argument is that online access delivered in the wrong way—the wrong machines, installed by the wrong vendor—can't do what needs to be done. "Successful access" to information is redefined to mean "access over the correct electronic system, which has been successfully installed: " which is further modified to mean the specific system installation that benefits Fidelity by meeting their timely, strategic, technical, and business system needs. It is important that no distinction is made between technical and business needs—technology is neither an issue nor a selling point. Online access is almost a byproduct of the correct installation and the improved performance of the high tech office.

Fidelity's senior vide-presidents are shown. Their earnest expressions, maturity, and wisdom are projected in a dramatic photograph. The reader is meant to identify with these men who have chosen BusinessLand services. They are visual evidence of Fidelity's good judgment in human resources and the high quality of BusinessLand's customers. Also, these fine men have chosen BusinessLand. (To understand some of the visual power of this ad, imagine, if you can, how this advertisement would have looked if they were a couple of goofy looking guys: what credibility would it have had then?) Since the referral object of the photography cannot be Fidelity, BusinessLand is borrowing Fidelity's credibility to add to its image. Split-second timing is mentioned in the headline, and the copy tells us that the installation was completed ahead of schedule. Read: Fidelity's men demand action and make quick but correct decisions to get the job done. In this context that means choosing BusinessLand for the job because BusinessLand is our kind of outfit, one that is like us.

IMPLICIT COPY   The advertisement was printed in black and white in full-page newspaper format. At that scale the faces were almost life size and the presentation was very dramatic and arresting. The type is crisp and clear; the whole effect is bold and classy.

AUDIENCES   The content is an appeal to systems managers or CFOs to use BusinessLand computer centers for correcting, updating, or expanding their systems. The advertisement targets the high level corporate decision maker as the buyer of choice who is even visualized by the Fidelity executives. He or she is meant to be impressed by BusinessLand as Fidelity's choice for this hairy project. The message is "we do it now" for the "best of companies." The needs-gap addressed is the systemic problem of the high tech office. BusinessLand is positioned as the leader in project implementation and business problem solving for other leaders.

COMPARISON OF THE SHARK/WANG AND BUSINESS-LAND ADVERTISEMENTS   Both are courting the same level of customer and both are using online as a "problem leader" to get the attention of specific initial buyers. Their goals are different however. Shark is repositioning the market through a turnkey program stressing advanced technology. BuisnessLand is positioning by stressing the company it keeps. Both advertisements project online access as a problem within the larger problem of the high tech office. Both offer the same two-step formula: first, fix the high tech office and, second, get the information results one wants from the improved online access. This scheme recognizes the initial buyer's problems by focusing on the management paradoxes of high tech systems. More importantly, both advertisers recognize that the customer thinks about these issues in an outwardly directed manner, moving from his personal and corporate environment to the world at large, and their advertisements link up productively with his mind-set.

5.10. The Personal Versus the Abstract in Positioning

EXPLICIT COPY   This is an advertisement for aspiring people. The prospect for the Dow Jones service is labeled a contender, and serious contenders can't be handicapped by a lack of equities data. This is a tired shopworn copy premise. Appeals like "It is easy to get in touch with us" are changed into ring, playing field, or locker room clichés like "You probably won't even break a sweat." The copy is right out of the witless chatter on the Super Bowl broadcast. But all is redeemed: the language of the advertisement is tired but the typography and art are new minted coin.

IMPLICIT COPY   The type is elegant and forceful: the drawing is crinkly and tentative. The type is dense: the art is airy. They play off each other's inherent expressions, with the contrasts heightening their best qualities. The whole advertisement pulses to the same contrasting internal beat. The final result is a witty magazine advertisement printed excellently on slick white paper that enhances the graphic fineness of the lines in the drawing and the shape and clarity of the type elements.

AUDIENCE   The model of the user is one who knows the market, is not cyberphobic, will profit from information, and deserves a winning edge. The advertisement puts the blame for any shortcomings in his performance on the lack of timely data to support his decision

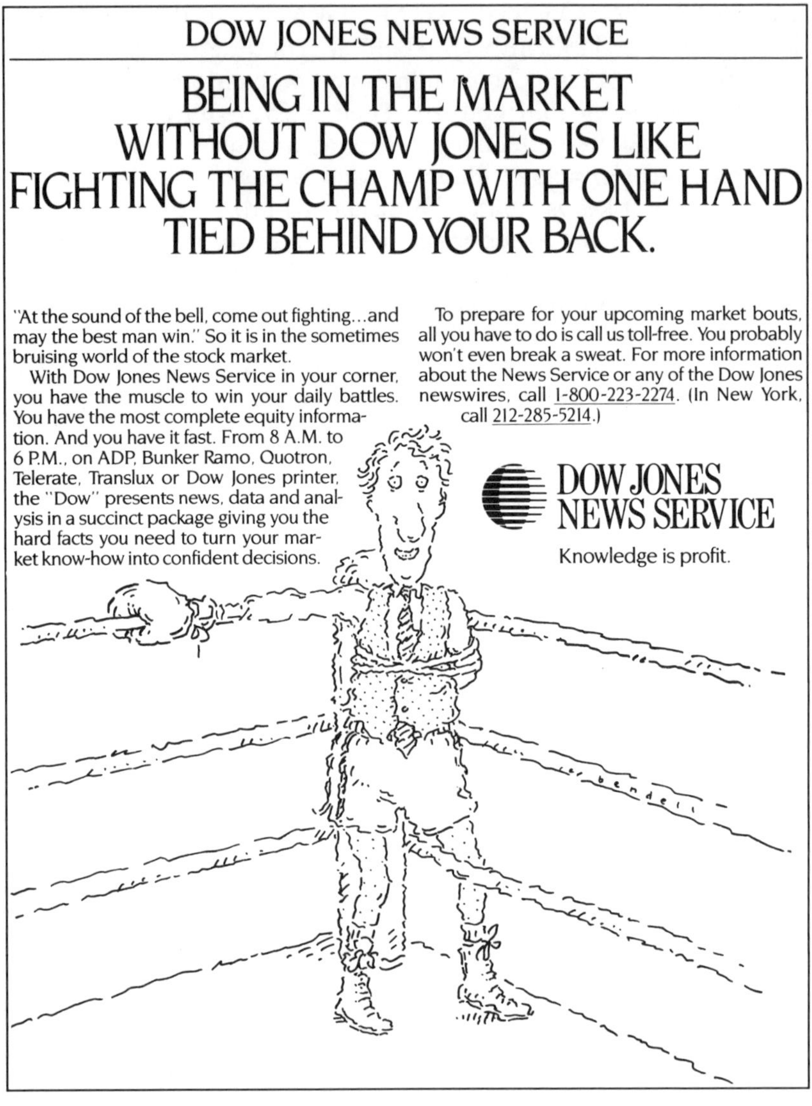

Figure 5.9. An advertisement by Dow Jones News Service.

making. The art depicts a wimp who may, or may not, stay to face the champ. The advertisement promises that Dow Jones will supply the muscle needed to win and that the subscriber does not even have to train for the "bout" (read: the service is easy to use and requires no special training).

EXPLICIT COPY   This is an advertisement about being the leader in the large sense in the knowledge market. It is almost corporate image advertising with secondary references to products. The position taken is that McGraw-Hill is the overall leader in information technologies in the whole knowledge market. The headlines and copy stress commitment to quality and the ability to create access to large databases. No specific product is mentioned by brand but several are alluded to. The positioning is well supported by crisp, clean, effective, and convincing copy.

At the image level things are coming unwired in this advertisement's message. The image chosen to support the copy is cybernetic to the nth degree; humankind and system are shown as literally merged. A giant's hand moves the cyborgs to their appointed places on a memory and processor board. The visual idea involves an attempt to make the board a complex symbol for organizational design, technology, the information environment, and the world at large. The illustration ends up being contextally confusing to the reader because it depicts "connecting," which is the wrong issue if the subhead is believed. The right leadership issue is "new ways," defined as breakthrough applications of technology to information problems.

Not even a cyberphile could easily accept this seemingly orders-from-on-high style of "connecting" as it is shown here in the cause of better communications, and the cyberphobe would be horrified. What reader could identify with the gloomy cyborgs or would willingly want to share their fate? They are the antithesis of the active decision maker spoken of in the copy. As depicted here, they mirror the worst fears of the social critics of the information age.

IMPLICIT COPY   The advertisement is well presented graphically and well laid out for ease of reading and legibility. The illustration is well realized and printed in full, if somewhat harsh, colors.?

AUDIENCES   There are at least three estimates of who the buyers or general audience might be.

(1) *Product segment.* Readers who can identify with the off-screen giant and who are either corporate or organizational executives (CFOs?) and who have initial buyers (like MIS managers) reporting to them—the cyborgs would then be the initial buyers; or remote initial buyers with users and endusers reporting to them—the cyborgs would then be the users or endusers.

(2) *Organizational segment.* Readers who can identify with the action of the giant, which is either "connecting" people to systems, or "connecting" people and systems into networks and organizations.

Figure 5.10.　An Advertisement by McGraw-Hill. *Reproduced by permission of McGraw-Hill, Inc.*

p them make decisions with ater confidence in an increasly complex world.

McGraw-Hill is already employ₁ this technology, for example, deliver instant access to informaη on corporate and municipal ₁ds for the financial community. provide on-line distribution economic data on construction ₁nds and potential. And to make : world's largest private collection economic data bases respon-

sive to the specific needs of business and government planners.

In these ways and more, technology is helping us make otherwise overwhelming amounts of information more valuable by making it more useful and instantly accessible. And by providing new

channels of information distribution with selectivity and built-in search capabilities.

These new applications of communications technology are a natural extension of McGraw-Hill's basic charter: to provide people with the information they need. Information that leads to action.

McGraw-Hill, Inc., 1221 Avenue of the Americas, New York, New York 10020.

Information that leads to action.

They might be initial buyers, users, endusers, or corporate/organizational managers.

(3) *Corporate image segment.* Readers who see the hand as McGraw-Hill itself, acting to connect people and systems, and who see themselves, if at all, as one of the people being connected; they would view the cyborgs as themselves or their superiors or peers.

No model of the participant is clear enough, and defining one is a difficult analytical task, taking far longer than the average reader is willing to spend with most advertisements (3.6 seconds). A simple test reveals the issue. If the people in the advertisement were depicted as standing on the memory blocks instead of being imbedded in them, the advertisement would be more acceptable because information freedom would be honored. If the hand was shown holding the block, not the person, while plugging it into the board (and the person was standing on the block), the giant could be read as perfecting the utility of the system for a free people. This test shows that the communications issue is in the literal translation of the pun into an illustration. The illustration adds no new information to the advertisement. Instead it blurs the advertisement by undermining the moorings of the copy. The needs-gap addressed is prestige.

COMPARISON OF THE DOW JONES AND McGRAW-HILL ADVERTISEMENTS   These advertisements demonstrate that success in visual representation is critical. In the Dow Jones's advertisement, tired copy is reinvigorated by illustration, layout, and typography into a witty success. In the McGraw-Hill advertisement, the meaning of the copy is blurred by the illustration. The difference is conceptual. In the Dow Jones advertisement the typography and illustration add new information that builds the idea and heightens the theme. McGraw-Hill's literal reiteration of the pun blurs the sense and focus of the advertisement, adding nothing conceptually and holding back the copy—indeed, it would have been stronger without the illustration.

5.11. Pricing and Advertising

EXPLICIT COPY   Pricing determines marketing strategy. This service goes for the marketing win on subscriptions by giving password numbers to almost anyone who asks. Price is a pun in the headline that expands the message theme and sets the stage for making as little as possible of the fact that charges are incurred during use. The user is invited to subscribe to a system presented as having no price barriers to use. This tactic is based on the assumption that the user is confused and put off by procedural complexity and the imagined

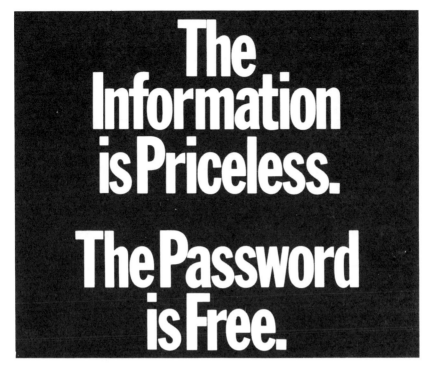

No one in personnel can put a price on good information — it is simply an essential part of the decision making process. But with so much information available in so many forms, it's hard to find exactly what you need.

Let Pergamon InfoLine help you!

One of the databases InfoLine holds is Management and Marketing Abstracts, a unique service designed to give you all the information you need on personnel and industrial relations as well as covering other important aspects of management and marketing. All available in the most convenient way possible — through a direct telephone link from any microcomputer in your office.

Now if you think this kind of facility sounds expensive, think again. InfoLine will issue you with your free password to our comprehensive store of data. There are no subscription charges and no hidden extras. You simply pay for what you use.

For further information and your free password, simply call us today on 01-377 4650 or return the coupon below. You'll also receive details of our free introductory search-time offer.

PERGAMON
INFO
LINE
The Search is Over

IPM

Name _____

Address _____

Return to: Pergamon InfoLine Ltd, Marketing Department, 12 Vandy Street, London EC2A 2DE   Telephone:01-377 4650   Telex:8814614

Figure 5.11.   An advertisement from InfoLine.

high costs of online services. The appeal, expressed beautifully in the headline type, is that InfoLine cuts through all of that in the user's behalf. The free benefit is priceless information obtained at little or no effort.

IMPLICIT COPY   The bold headlines play effectively on each other, forming the graphic element of the advertisement that holds the reader's attention. The text is presented in display type and is easy to read. The whole presentation is direct and simple. The ideas are carried through clearly and forcefully with plain means.

AUDIENCES   The users.

EXPLICIT/IMPLICIT COPY   Textline is positioned as the "hassle free" online service and costs are represented as being totally managed by their pricing policy of fixed annual fees. The needs-gap addressed in this advertisement is the information perceptions of the underequipped neophyte user. Equipment and translations are promised, and every other detail is spelled out and included in a turnkey European-service package. The advertisement presents eight features and details of the service that outline the form of the package. Each feature statement is followed by a benefit statement directed at some interest of the user, and is placed directly beneath the feature statement in italic type. (Five of the "benefits" are stated as benefits, the other three are stated as features, and the benefits have to be interpolated from them.) The copy is terse. The layout of the page is like an online service screen. At the bottom of the advertisement is a usable coupon with a telephone number.

AUDIENCES   Initial buyers.

COMPARISON OF INFOLINE AND TEXTLINE   The similarities of the two company names mandate a need to differentiate the two in the market so that the buyer doesn't get mixed up. Each advertisement is directed to the interests of its targeted audience. Both advertisements employ about the same means of representation, but the emotional appeal of InfoLine is more dramatic and imaginative, as it should be since it is directed at the user. TextLine's is suitably rational for the initial buyer. InfoLine succeeds in differentiating itself from TextLine. Its appeal connects to the mind-set of the user in a productive way that TextLine's cannot: in both cases, however, the policy of reducing complexity and delivering outstanding value reaches into the center of the stubborn problem of user cyberphobia. Recognition by the reader of the approach to these factors overcomes and differentiates the strong representational similarities.

Figure 5.12. An advertisement by TextLine. *Courtesy of Finsbury Data Services.*

Figure 5.13. An advertisement by McCarthy Information Services. *Courtesy of Financial Times Information Services Division.* Produced by Christopher Ogg Associates Ltd.

5.12. "Positioning is What You Do to the Mind of the Prospect. That Is, You Position the Product in the Mind of the Prospect."[7]

EXPLICIT COPY   This campaign may succeed in repositioning the entire idea of online use by its keen understanding that "positioning is not what you do to a product." This campaign creates "a new location in the mind of the user." McCarthy hammers away at a new problem for the online user, namely, that the user's managers' expectations of the user have risen as a result of the user's access to an online system. The advertisement asserts on management's behalf that proactive information searching is now a standard part of anyone's work if he has access to an online system. The copy argues and the picture shows that any user who doesn't think in these terms is out of step with the world, and radically out of step with his organizational responsibilities.

The new position may be stated as: access to an online information utility changes the context of judgment about both success and information relevance by promoting the "formerly obscure, and therefore unknowable" into the "immediately knowable" cateogry, and thereby instantly raising the stakes of its worth.

A complex dramatic incident is presented. A user is in rueful retreat from his boss's scorn. He is shown in the act of being expelled from a huge office by his superior (who also uses the McCarthy system, and, significantly, does so more proactively than the user does). The scene is staged in a campy parody of the German expressionist photographic idiom of the 1920's, memorable mainly for its distortion of visual perspective. Proactive searching is evoked but never mentioned directly. Its meanings are made startlingly vivid by a combination of expressions. Particularly subtle and effective is the Voice, a kind of Greek chorus; the headline is uttered (off stage) by a voice sympathizing with the user; it is voicing his self-pity. The Voice adds a new notion (the second headline) to the interior monologue. This statement shows that the user has perhaps learned the new rule that motivates his boss's concern over "important" competitive information.

IMPLICIT COPY   The overall visual density of the advertisement is risky. The whole area is covered with type, pictures, logo, and coupons with the visual result that it appears too "gray," lacking in striking visual emphasis. The text paragraphs discuss the features of the system. A somewhat usable coupon with phone numbers is enclosed.

AUDIENCES   The user is challenged to use online proactively in defense of the company and his own position, and a hands-on initial buyer is given permission to berate those users who don't. Both are market targets, and this is one of the few electronic publishing advertisements of the many I have studied that deals successfully with both buyers and users.

COMPARISON OF THE INFOLINE AND McCARTHY ADVERTISEMENTS   The user is the prospect in both advertisements, and the factual content and benefits of the two services are approximately the same. McCarthy, however, has "invented" a new benefit, the ability to stay one step ahead of one's boss. No one would like being in the situation dramatized by the McCarthy advertisement, and everyone would enjoy being in the situation of knowing what one should know, when one should know it. That vivid benefit is easy to remember. InfoLine's appeal is based on price and ease of use but has the drawback of not allowing any room for evocative situations like the one in the McCarthy advertisement. InfoLine does tick off its point about costs and service benefits rationally and unmistakably. The strength of this appeal may be that it reaches the user very well indeed. The strength of the McCarthy advertisement is that the user and the hands-on initial buyer each can learn something positive (depending on one's point of view) about corporate survival and success, an appeal to a younger aspiring user audience. Both firms get the marketing win with the initial buyer, of course; but McCarthy rightly assumes that they have to go far beyond pricing to win a permanent place in the user's mind.

5.13. Global Marketing in Advertising

In the online industry there are global marketers who have a global information style. Their advertising exploits their wide-ranging awareness to color and strengthen their image, appeals, and products. It infuses their work with the marketing signature of a global player. These marketers tackle the data and information needs-gap that is common to multinational and global enterprises, namely, having online information on hand in time to act profitably on distant, widespread, unconnected, fast-changing events involving many players and their interests.

EXPLICIT COPY   The Reuter Monitor Bonds Database is a new product introduction. "Stay ahead in the bonds market with comprehensive listings and real time information" is the theme of the advertisement. Edge for the bond trader is the message. The new service comes over existing Reuter Monitor screens already installed in the trading room, so the sales goal is adoption of the new service by current users. The global point that Reuters stresses is that the system was designed by studying the information needs of bond dealers and their customers, which means working closely with a large complex international market. A trading room is shown with five men hard at work. The details of the room indicate global awareness and technology sufficient to keep on top of a world market. The lighting dramatizes the intensity of the men and glamourizes their equipment. There is a sense of intense quiet, a concentration on the flux of the market. In this photograph men dominate their machines and control them. Screens show a stream of data flowing in, and the postures of the men show that they are responding and participating in the action. They are in charge. They look like men who are winning in the bonds market; they embody the statement at the end of the copy, "If you want to stay ahead in the bonds market . . ." (be like these men). It is at this point that a fascinating and useful ambiguity emerges. The men can be read as the reader's colleagues or staff, or alternatively as the competition. If they are read as staff, they are great staff with the best technology to do their job. If they are read as the competition, the reader had better get the Reuter Database right now.

IMPLICIT COPY   This two-page, four-color magazine advertisement is perfect in every presentation detail, and the quality of the photography is outstanding. The high level of implicit quality fits perfectly with Reuters' case.

AUDIENCES   In this sales situation there are two possible buyer audiences. The user might ask for the product so he can do a better job, or the product might be chosen for the user by a remote initial buyer. Both customers are visualized and appealed to in this advertisement. The user, shown four times in the photo, is highly dramatized and flattered. A remote buyer or supervisor is shown standing at the back of the console monitoring trades, but he can be discounted as a main participant in the appeal because the coupon is directed at the user. He may be there just to remind the user that he is someone to be pleased by the users' performance because a remote initial buyer of a system of this size would have a customer representative who would personally introduce all new products to him. This advertisement attempts to get the sale started by upward pressure initiated by the user.

EXPLICIT COPY   Telerate's world is both market and database. Access is promised in selective compression "on one [screen] page."

Stay ahead in the

The new Reuter Monitor Bonds Database is a natural addition to the range of specialist financial services created by Reuters to assist the market operator.

It gives instant access to key facts and market makers' prices on a current range of over 3,200 Eurobonds which will be expanded as new bonds are issued.

COMPREHENSIVE LISTINGS

No extra equipment beyond the dealer's existing Reuter Monitor screen and keyboard is necessary. With a few key strokes, an investor or trader obtain three listings: comprehensiv details of the issue; price data inclu average closing prices, the yearly lows and four yield calculations; anc list of up to 24 market makers who made a market in that bond in any 2 hour period.

REAL TIME INFORMATION

Tap in the market makers' cod receive further pages of informatic their prices in real time.

Designed after considerable

Figure 5.14.   An advertisement by Reuters.

)onds market

:arch with both bond dealers and stors, the Reuter Monitor Bonds abase provides extensive, easily-ievable data at a modest price. It is one of the new products Reuters is eloping as part of a programme to ide new and improved services to t the increasingly sophisticated ds of this rapidly growing market.

So if you want to stay ahead in the ds market, get in touch with Reuters. the coupon or contact your local ter office.

REUTERS

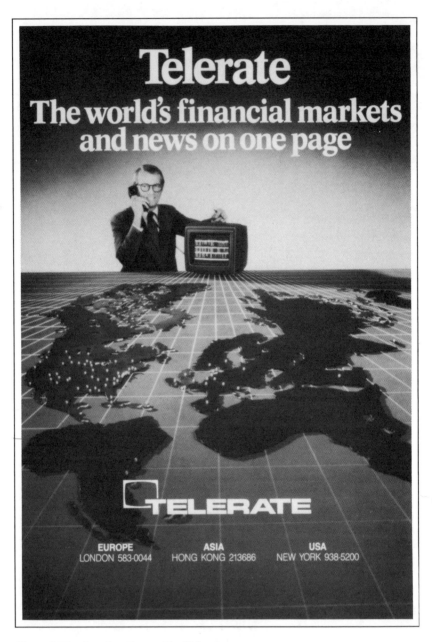

Figure 5.15.   An advertisement by Telerate.

The headline is the copy; it also defines the image on the screen. The phone numbers of three international offices are given at the bottom of the advertisement, two of which are located on the Atlantic basin with the other in Asia. Telerate is a global marketer with a global product. The world map looks like a war room situational map and, like the Telerate database, the advertisement shows the world on one page. The man is the "general" in charge of the war. This projection places the Atlantic basin in the center. Grids passing under the land masses extend to the horizon converging on the line of the terminal. The page display on the screen and the grid lines are analogous by color. (The grid symbolizes the communications nets that feed the Telerate database.) The man by the terminal uses the terminal with the same aplomb with which he uses a telephone. The tone of the advertisement is crepuscular; twilight purples and oranges suggest evening. The afterglow radiates behind the man to indicate the setting sun and, perhaps, to remind the reader that the timing of the world markets changes with the rotation of the earth.

IMPLICIT COPY   The advertisement is well printed in a one-page magazine format in four colors. The overall effect is a little muddy and soft, but that is due to the color scheme used in the design of the illustration. Every type element is legible and readable even though they are reversed through the background. The total effect is not dramatic.

AUDIENCES   This advertisement sells to the highest ranking user. He is not cyberphobic. He is as at ease with the technology as he is with monitoring a far-flung and changing situation; in fact, he is shown as handling world-level decisions with ease, even charm. He monitors the world on one page and is confident of the accuracy and timeliness of the report. The appeal projected by this advertisement is personal mastery and technical and market sophistication, a top-level user appeal. The user shown here is also a high level investor or executive because he can use summary information, a fact that automatically indicates his rank at the top of the data pyramid (where summaries are used exclusively).

   Note: Both of these advertisements build a global marketing image that is strongly reinforced and confirmed by their actions in the market. Global marketing philosophy holds that the world is becoming one market and should be marketed to as such. Both advertisements show men who are used to that idea and take it in stride, just as the advertisers and their products and services do. The global theme is that a combination of the right technology and the right database can handle the international market challenge. In the Reuters advertisement, part of that message is conveyed by the naturalistic picture of a technical environment and the serious tone of the advertisement. The database benefits are inferred from the postures and attitudes of the men as they win in the market and from the copious display of data that enables them to do so. The message that a world-class online service delivers the right database for international trading is conveyed in every aspect of the art and copy, but nowhere more clearly than in the idea that the system was designed by study and analysis of the international market and its international players.

This example shows the evolving principles of product building in high tech marketing. By definition, only a world-class online service could do an international high tech financial feedback-loop study on bond trading and then design and build a database to fit the findings. Few would or could even think in those terms unless they were global players themselves. Technologists can always make up some kind of database, but the market fit might be off by a mile without trader and customer data to shape it—this is the world marketing viewpoint in action, shaping database technology to make the product marketable.

The product itself is an excellent way of showing one's credentials in a world market and as a global marketer, a tactic that is not lost on Telerate. In their advertisement they have made the world visible to demonstrate that it is manageable and knowable, and, through the use of the grid lines, known to Telerate. Information flows from all over the world to the user via the Telerate database and network technology. Impressive as that is, the real message isn't technical because it isn't the technology that makes it possible (technology just makes it feasible). What makes it possible is Telerate's intellectual overview of world markets combined with an understanding of their customers' information needs expressed through technology. In that sense both of these advertisements achieve some corporate advertising goals as well as marketing goals (Telerate more so than Reuters) because as a marketing device they reveal their corporate reach and consciousness to the reader—a powerful set of image-building messages in this context that won't be wasted on those readers with similar business goals and information needs, attitudes, and cosmopolitan values.

5.14. Corporate Communications Strategies in Support of Corporate Goals and Marketing Programs

The goal of corporate campaigns in support of marketing is to foster and increase buyer awareness and acceptance. The gain sought is more buyer's recognition of the company's name and product/service images, a gain that makes sales easier to obtain and clients easier to keep. Sometimes this is done with ideas; on other occasions people, markets, products, and services are featured. The latter approach is often used when the seller is dominant in his market, because dominance is comforting, attractive, and persuasive for many buyers. Corporate advertising in support of marketing must fit in with and express the goals of the whole marketing communications program. (Public relations in support of marketing is discussed in chapter 6.)

Not just marketing issues are addressed in corporate advertising. Marketing must be aware of the program and make sure that it supports marketing goals where it can and should. (Corporate advertising should never be paid for from the marketing budget or be administered by marketing—marketing has better ways to spend its money and use its time.) Seven corporate issues are often addressed by advertising programs:

Acquisitions, Divestitures, and Takeovers

"Big business in America is overhauling itself and its operations faster than at any time since World War II."[8] The goal is increased profits from slimmed down or augmented operations. Corporate advertising is used to maintain consistent company images in an era of widespread change, to reassure stockholders, customers, and suppliers, to introduce the new organizations and product lines as they come into being, and frequently by both sides to tell their stories during contested corporate takeovers.

Bond Performance, Investor Relations, Price-Earnings Ratio, and Capital Requirements

Bonds have become very complex financial instruments as the types in use and the range of applications have multiplied. Organizations using bonds and other national and international financial instruments and equities will need expert counsel on managing their relations with investors and financiers. At one time it was thought price-earnings ratios were a critical index and that an unfavorable change was a signal for advertising. Few hold that view today because corporate advertising is too expensive and powerful a tool to be used just to change the perspectives of a few key analysts. (Programs for analysts have come into use that do not employ advertising in any way, and are both stronger and cheaper as a consequence.) Generally, good financial performance indicates a lowered need for corporate advertising: poor or standard performance may indicate the need for a campaign directed at adjusting overall impressions.

Business-to-Business Relations

Corporate advertising is strongly indicated if an online organization has a poor image in the publishing industry itself, with technical peers and competitors, with publishers or suppliers, or in R & D. All are often-consulted sources of important secondary PR information about the organization that circulates widely and influentially among buyers and the trade press: ideally, all of these communities should be at the very least neutral and at best enthusiastic about the company, its management, staff, pricing, services, products, markets, and future.

Factors Arising from Company Size and Organizational Complexity

Most online organizations are small businesses of relative simplicity, easy to understand by most audiences. Corporate advertising is useful in building and maintaining single memorable images for large complex organizations whose actions, product lines, and policies are unrecognizable or misunderstood by staff, subsidiaries, the public at large, and corporate and investor audiences. Market dominance in a key sector of the market by a small firm may provide an excellent platform for limited programs aimed at that market and allied sectors.

Branded Product and Service Lines

If the company and its product and service lines all carry the same corporate name and mark, and are well established and identified in their major markets, corporate advertising will not be needed in support of marketing as much as it will be by those firms who need to be more strongly identified because their products and services are marketed under other, individual or differing brand or corporate names. In the online industry product and service lines are relatively simple, low priced, and frequently purchased (by the user). In industries where these conditions occur corporate advertising is rarely used: Procter & Gamble, Lever Brothers, and Bristol Myers are examples.

Employee Relations and Personnel Recruitment

Neither is an issue in the online industry. The companies are attractive places to work. Most have fewer than 250 employees, and the work is not labor intensive. Advertising is not warranted under these conditions.

Corporate Image

Corporate image advertising is a global design. Its benefits blanket the organization, its products, services, staff, customers, and audiences. When used well it reveals, sharpens, and enhances understanding of the organization's collective mystique, world view, personality, style, power, and achievements. The luster of a creative campaign adheres to everything internally, adding to awareness, morale, and pride. Sometimes the benefits sought are intangible but profound; it is the one communications arena where many corporations choose to speak freely, even majestically or poetically, about historical, economic, social and scientific truth (or myth), accomplishments, and beliefs as a way of establishing image by association. Identity itself is becoming an ever more important business asset in a complex world, densely packed as it is with rapidly changing faceless international corporations and institutions, with alphabet names and Panama registry.

COSTS

The expense of a campaign can be so high that it must deal with important corporate issues and audiences. No average of the annual United States or British corporate advertising expenditures would be significant here or establish a useful guide line for any online corporation to follow, because each corporation responds to its own unique mix of industry and corporate issues.

NAMES

Advertising and public relations agency arguments aside, who can measure in dollars or pounds what a better or different corporate image is worth to a corporation until long after the fact? "Largely because of increased merger and acquisition activity last year, corporate name changes reached a new high. . . . The total in the United States alone was 1,382, a 32.8% gain [over 1985]. . . ."[9] Logically and practically, every business person knows that image counts in the market because buyers respond to well-crafted images; they help them make comparative judgments among goods and services. In the online industry, beefing up corporate image may help sales and use where (1) the products and services are new or are not distinguished by innate differences in the databases or services; (2) the market is international or wide and varied; and (3) the bulk of earnings is drawn from repeated use. Market positioning is the final determinant for choosing corporate advertising concepts in support of marketing.

Notes

1. P. Muller and R. Wilson, *Pricing Policies for Parallel Publishing* (Oxford: Elsevier, 1985), 1, 29.
2. L. Salerno, "What Happened to the Computer Revolution?," *Harvard Business Review* 63, no. 6 (November–December 1985):137–38.

3. W. Davidow, *Marketing High Technology* (New York: Free Press, 1986), 197, 89.
4. A. Ries and J. Trout, *Positioning: The Battle for Your Mind* (New York: McGraw-Hill, 1981), 3.
5. R. McKenna, *The Regis Touch* (Reading: Addison-Wesley, 1985), 35–50.
6. Davidow, *Marketing*.
7. Salerno, "What Happened . . . ?"
8. L. Wayne, "Merger Mania," *New York Times*, 20 December 1986.
9. P. Dougherty, "Corporate Name Changes Set Mark," *New York Times*, 5 January 1987.

6

INCREASING MARKETING EFFICIENCY BY EXPANSION OF THE MARKETING TOOL MIX

PRESSURE ON MARKETING'S TRADITIONAL TOOLS

Marketing is being assigned new or expanded missions. Especially challenging are programs to improve market share in the secondary and tertiary markets. Unlike traditional online marketing in prime markets, marketing costs in the secondary and tertiary markets are bounded by the expected return, a limiting condition. The problem is in the lower revenue potential/sale in these markets. Marketing success is measured by efficiently capturing share with a high volume of sales.

The tools discussed in this chapter exploit the internal and external opportunities available for increasing marketing efficiency in marketing programs, in sales and marketing communications programs, and, last, but not least, in the market itself. After maximizing the productivity of all currently used marketing and communications programs, marketing managers can weigh their opportunities to use four more marketing tools. They are (1) market research and competitive analysis, (2) direct marketing, (3) direct telemarketing, and (4) public relations in support of marketing programs. Each is examined below.

6.1. Market Research and Competitive Analysis

Consider the many advantages to an online marketing organization from investing in and perfecting the use of market research and competitive analysis.

No United States online organization has a professional market research department; most do not even have an individual trained in market research or in its interpretation and application to marketing issues. Some have drifted in that direction through the personal inclination of the marketing director or in response to some temporary market necessity; most do some limited market research and use market and marketing consultants from time to time.

Market research is not well accepted in the online industry. On the management side of the house, market research is just another marketing expense, probably an unnecessary one that can be ill afforded. On the technical side of the house (where technology is often viewed as the growth driver of the online industry), many find it hard not to dismiss the contributory value of market research; market research reports are, to them, fuzzy sociological stuff that can't be factored into the technology anywhere. Pragmatists on all sides of the online house write it off as pure high-altitude theory, an esoteric function dealing in the stratosphere of marketing ideas—with no practical application at sea level.

What is being overlooked is that a professionally conducted market research program in an online company could pose, study, and answer important marketing and competitive questions. Answers to some or all of the following marketing questions would help in building greater sales efficiency and support revenue growth plans better than "informed" intuition, technical dogma, past history, or consulting engagements.

Industry Analysis

Watching the activities of the online industry as a whole: economic factors, market factors, technological factors that will or may affect the industry. What print publishers are doing with regard to electronic publishing, either on their own or through others, is an example of an industry issue that definitely bears watching.

Business Analysis

Watching business factors that may affect the organization. This narrows the consideration of industry analysis to those factors that will have a direct effect on the specific organization such as personal consumer credit trends or the rate of personal investment in microcomputer systems, and so on.

Competitive Analysis

Tracking the competition. Reviewing product offerings, content, software, marketing/sales strategies, collateral materials, recruiting of staff, attendance at trade shows, advertising, etc. Constantly making an effort to estimate the revenues and margins of competitors. In short, everything that can be legally and ethically known about the competition.

Pricing Analysis

A subfunction of competitive analysis, but important enough to be a separate program. Complete analysis of pricing and all of the other factors within the company's market that bear on pricing: elasticity of the markets served, customer reaction to pricing, cancellation analysis after price changes, regret analysis before price changes, estimates of the effect of various price levels on the growth of market share, etc.

Market Analysis

Who is in the market populations served by the service? What are their characteristics? Where are they? How can they be reached more effectively? What is the cost/benefit of the various methods of reaching the market. How should a target market be segmented, and what are the different tactics needed to reach and serve the segments?

Customer Analysis

Monitoring current customers, especially the top 20 percent. Most online organizations have a wealth of data on current users that is rarely exploited for the good of the company. Of the current customers, who is using the system most? Why? Which parts of the online system's databases are most popular, and why? From which part of the service is most of the company's revenue derived, and why? Where are most of the company's gross margins derived, and why?

Product Design

Market research is the best tool available today for understanding and getting the needs and requirements of the customer built into marketing and customer communications, knowledge products, technology, and the service system.

To summarize, the questions above show that the goal of a strong market research program is to find the most efficient way for the online organization to make its revenue goal. Research activities of this type have little to do with "high-altitude" issues at this stage of industry maturity and market development. Most of the work would be at "sea level" on practical marketing and sales issues. If a market research program is properly directed, it lowers marketing expense, helps assure that what is being spent on technology and marketing is spent more wisely, and directly adds to revenues through improved marketing efficiency and sales execution. The actual work is prosaic, such as compiling listings of prospects based on marketing's informed understanding of the possible markets; defining the profiles of past, present, and potential good customers and determining which new customers can be sold and supported cheaply and which can't. It can provide a rational basis for some marketing decisions on tactical marketing and sales plans. Its recording function can create a history of marketing programs from which a great deal can be learned to improve marketing performance. It is a multipurpose marketing tool for learning from the past, for applying market information today, and for preparing for the future of the technology, the products, the marketing program, the company, and the industry.

6.2. Direct Marketing

Consider the many advantages to an online marketing organization from investing in and perfecting the use of its direct mail operations.

Direct marketing means direct mail in the online industry. Direct mail is used haphazardly in online marketing programs at the current time. If its use were improved it would contribute directly to greater sales and marketing efficiency. Generally, direct mail has emerged as one of the best of the basic direct marketing tools, and has found growing success in large consumer marketing applications in many different markets in the United States and Great Britain, particularly those where millions of units can be mailed, where samples are large enough to test reliably for what works best, and where all elements of the entire campaign can be tuned and retuned to achieve the best response at the lowest cost/sale ratio.

The online industry has little, if any, need for mass programs at this stage of industry development and maturity for the following reasons. Computer use is not widespread in the same sense that use of soap or soup is; online systems are not yet idiot proof, a very serious problem that limits their usefulness and attractiveness to wide populations; online charges are high ticket items by mass audience standards; charges are variable and therefore hard to compare with the prices of competing systems; many target markets are extremely difficult and expensive to catalog (at the proper name-and-position level) and would fail to reach the cost/benefit threshold of a full-fledged mass mailing program.

Much is being done throughout the industry, but none of the direct mail efforts can use all of the functional and analytical techniques available for mass audiences. The industry has adopted a direct mail methodology suitable to its purse and markets. It is used for a number of marketing missions and valued as a low cost method of marketing and customer communications. The marketing value of direct mail is that it shows products and their benefits in a personal context that leads directly to a sale or establishes the preconditions to a sale. Most direct mail uses a well-understood sales convention, namely, a built-in sales technology for completing the sale autonomously (a coupon or toll-free number, or both). The goal of any online sale is to obtain a level of continuity over time. Ideally, the customer commits to the service for a period of time or on an open-ended basis, and when the pricing variables permit it, direct mail is very good at making this kind of sale. Direct mail works by making an advantageous offer (usually time limited) and giving a benefit in exchange for the acceptance of the offer (usually a price benefit such as a discount on time fees for some period or free online use, or it offers a premium, like a card-sized calculator). Price and premium, the traditional direct mail offer elements, fit the scheme of obtaining a buyer commitment with its promise of continuity in online service use.

Direct mail fits certain marketing needs of online industry and is widely used. It is a quick response tool to market opportunities or a counterpunch to the competition. When necessary, it is a fast and reliable, but limited, substitute for a sales call. The whole market can be reached by a single mailing, or the market can be segmented and reached segment by segment with different appeals at different times, as needed.

Mail programs require follow-up programs and must be carefully coordinated with how, when, and by whom the follow-up will take place. Records of return mail or calls guide follow-up. Planning must extend to detail: how the paper path will flow to order entry, how each telemarketing call will be logged and followed up, when electronic versus paper recording of the contract or sale will be used, etc. Planning eliminates extra cost (including the cost of staff time) and maximizes sales. (See "Telemarketing" below.)

To summarize, in order to be successful there are four factors that must be considered, planned and executed perfectly in direct mail, namely,

1. The aims of the campaign must be clear.
2. The market targets of direct mail must be predetermined (and in some case prequalified) and the final mailing list must be carefully selected and prepared on the basis of the campaign criteria.

3. In any campaign, direct mail is the dependent variable. The style and quality of a direct mail effort must be matched to the campaign goals and targets; the direct mail piece is rarely recyclable into another direct mail program; and its timing must be coordinated with all of the active elements in the campaign, for example, advertising, new product introductions, and sales tours, and with the right buying moment for the customer, if possible.

4. Detailed plans for effective follow-up to all responses returned by buyers or users must be in place with all of the personnel, technology, and materials pretested, ready, and geared properly to the anticipated work and response loads. Without follow-up plans that work, a direct mail effort is wasted energy and resources, and may well fail to support the campaign as a whole.

MISSIONS

There are many missions for direct mail programs, some of which fall under the control of major campaign tactics and many that do not.

To Test the Interest of a Market in a Current Product.

Direct mail would be sent to a broad list with a coupon return. An active response is expected from the reader. Since a 2 percent return is a solid response to a direct mail program, the interest of the market can be determined, in part, by the extent to which the response rate exceeds 2 percent.

To Increase Name Recognition for the Company or Service in the Market

This falls into the set of image-building and sales activities called "softening up the market." An attractive mailer is created that requires a passive response from the reader. Admiration or excitement are the aims. Programs of this type are most effective when each receiver gets several different pieces of mail on a staggered schedule. Of course, this kind of program had better be leading up to something big (e.g., an offer by mail or a sales call) that will, in its turn, cause the buyer to act. The effectiveness of "softening" programs is determined by indirect measures such as the subsequent sales results in markets where this technique is applied, compared to the sales results in markets where the technique is not applied. Even if the results must be taken on faith, marketing managers say that it works, particularly if the campaign is visually exciting and creative.

To Get a Salesperson Known in His Market

If the online company is one of the few that have direct salespeople (most United States and British companies do not), direct mail can be an excellent method to get the salesperson's name, address, and phone number known. This aim can be combined with other marketing and sales goals.

To Generate and Qualify Leads

A *lead* in sales parlance is anyone who has even a remote interest in the service. A *qualified lead* is anyone who has access to, owns, or uses a computer with a modem, or is an enduser of online information. Leads, at the time they are located by the seller, can be at any point along the buying curve (the range is from "not interested" to "just bought a second online service installation"): the further the lead is along the curve toward buying once or again, the more qualified and valuable the lead is to the seller. In most new markets there are easy sales to be had, and finding these leads should take top priority. Direct mail programs can help separate the "lookers" from the "buyers." To accomplish this aim some action on the part of the receiver, such as either sending a return coupon or making a phone call, has to occur. How the lead should be used and plans for follow-up activities depend on the quality of leads themselves.

To "Close" an Initial Sale

Direct mail can be used to close (conclude on the spot) initial sales. Its success as a closing tool varies directly with pricing. When the initial commitment the buyer has to make in signing the contract is large, direct mail will not be successful. Some online sales are perfect candidates for direct mail, namely, those where there is a token sign-up fee.

Build Support for a Successful Sale

In large organizations there are many influences on a sale. Direct mail can be used successfully to ensure that the bit players support the buy decision, or to make it seem as if there is a ground swell of support for purchasing online services.

Introduce New Customers to the Service

Often the buyer (particularly in business and organizational settings) is not the user or potential user of the service. An ongoing direct mail program can be used to introduce the users or potential users to the benefits of the service and to keep stimulating their use over the long term. It is the use building application of direct mail that is so poorly used in the industry at the present time and is the one tactic that holds, in my judgment, the key to the greatest untapped potential for growth. (See "Build Use Among Current Users", below.)

Find New Users

Once the service is contracted and in the early stages of use, particularly in a large organization or institutional setting, a direct mail program can be used to discover the other potential users of the system and get them headed toward becoming users. In one sense this is a lead generation tactic that yields prequalified users with access to the system.

Build Use Among Current Users

Direct mail can also be used to get current users to use the service more. Using this technique to build use is important to all online companies, regardless of pricing. The holder of the annual contract wants to get value from his investment; use is his payoff. The hourly subscriber needs to be encouraged to use more online time to get the benefits of use that assure that he will be returning to the terminal.

Build Search Request Volume from Indirect Users and the Endconsumers of Information

In large organizations where the service is the province of information specialists, direct mail can be used within the organization to increase the volume of requests to the information specialists. The direct mail program must be structured to assure that the requests getting back to the information specialists result in searches that your service can fulfill.

Maintain Image with Nonusers

In many large organizations, there are a number of people who are not users but who influence the future of the use of the service. They may be the original decision maker, staff in purchasing, those who pay the bill, or those whose budgets are charged with the expense of service use, and so on. Direct mail programs aimed at these "influentials" have the ultimate aim of keeping the organization as a customer. Benefits are featured exclusively in such programs.

Build Traffic at a Trade Show Booth (or Other Company Event)

Trade show booth attendance should be encouraged. Many trade shows have so many exhibitions and activities that attendees can't possibly see them all. Direct mail before the show (or any company event) can try to assure a steady flow of at least "suspects," if not prospects, at the booth.

PROGRAM GOALS

In general, too many direct mail campaigns are hampered by a lack of clarity, or by trying to do too much with one mailing. Rational goals are important for budgeting, designing the program and the sales materials, and measuring results.

Program goals might be stated as follows:

- To spend from $Y to $Z to produce and mail X,000 units, as many times as is needed, to generate 200 qualified leads, measured by winnowing every 1,000 response calls to an 800 number down to the best leads.

Or again:

- To spend $Z to produce and mail a one-time mailing of XX,000 units to professional peer and management audiences in Y market to generate an attendance of 1,000 at the Y market tradeshow booth, as measured by the count of those attendees who bring their direct mail coupons to the booth to exchange them for premium A.

MAILING LISTS

Selection and/or preparation of high quality mailing lists is important. The best list gets the best results, but it can be hard to know which list is best and to estimate what it will produce. Specific goals can be met by direct mail, if the right list is available or can be constructed, not the other way around. The cost, availability, and applicability of mailing lists often determines the campaign, a common upside-down practice. For example, a direct mail campaign aimed at closing sales is useless unless the list has a high proportion of people who make purchase decisions. If acquisition of the best list is not possible, reconsider the campaign or adopt new goals. To do it the other way around is a poor way to run a campaign, because the indiscriminate buying of, and mailing to, inferior lists is the express train to high costs and low marketing efficiency. This practice leads some marketers to blame the direct mail medium for their failures and not the unwise and costly execution of a specific program.

BLIND LISTS

Many commercial mailing lists are prepared with no specific addressees' names, or they are addressed to a position within an organization. These are low productivity lists for online marketing programs because the small percentage of this class of "blind" mail that gets delivered to anyone at all, rarely gets delivered to the right person from the seller's point of view. If it should happen to arrive on the right person's desk, the appeal is not pointed enough to generate a response for a product or service like electronic database searching (keep in mind that there are real exceptions to this rule for other products in other industries). The best list is one prepared by a careful and ambitious sales person or expert market research specialist who has been personally collecting leads in his or her territory or market.

THE LAND'S END PROBLEM

Of course, the more personalized and pinpointed a list is, the more successful the campaign will be (if all of the other variables are in place). If the online service is one that requires personalized instruction, or sales are made through an account representative's call after the initial sale is completed, a mailing list for getting initial sales should always be partitioned by the sales and instruction department's geographic responsibility. There is no point in sending mail all the way to Land's End, if the travel and communications cost of making and servicing the sale are higher than the total revenue the company can ever earn from the account.

A HYPOTHETICAL CASE OF A MAJOR MAILING PROGRAM

This case demonstrates that researching the market variables at the planning stages of a direct mail program is a method of gaining an understanding of the attitudes and buying patterns in the market, and that when the research findings are applied to the direct mail program, cost drops and efficiency rises.

Assume the following program suppositions: (1) that the market is United States physicians, and (2) that the marketing aim is Y qualified leads for online services identified by direct mail in thirty working days, at a cost between $XX,000 and $XXX,000. It follows:

- Since very good lists already exist for the 500,000 doctors in the United States, it is possible to mail all of them for between $XXX,000 and $X,XXX,000.
- Market research would show that some specific medical specialties are more prone to buy high tech products and automated support services than others.

- The lists of 500,000 doctors can be subdivided by the relevant specialties, which are assumed, on the basis of market indicators, to be much better prospects.
- The nonspecialists doctors are dropped from the market population.

Marketing efficiency has improved and overall costs have been reduced by truncation and subdivision of the market. Have we considered everything that can be done? Overall efficiency goes up more and mailing costs go down if:

- The remaining list is partitioned into smaller, more manageable, homogeneous buyer groups, each of which would be addressed very efficiently by a version of the mailer expressly suited to their medical specialty vis-à-vis their relationship to computers. For example,

  1. those (by medical specialty) who own or have access to a personal computer would get version A
  2. those (by medical specialty) who actually use a personal computer would get version B
  3. those (by medical specialty) who already own or have access to a modem-equipped computer would get version C
  4. those (by medical specialty) who already use a modem-equipped computer would get version D

- The remaining qualfied doctors are juggled to fit the geographic realities of assigned sales territories and the locations of instruction centers (if these conditions apply).

Despite the costs of preparing and managing the mailing of four versions of the mailer, all the cost savings actions dictated by market research may well have brought overall costs down to the cost goal of between $XX,000 and $XXX,000, and marketing efficiency has soared since the leads obtained by the direct mail program are the best possible candidates for sales.

PERSONALIZED LETTER CAMPAIGNS, A SPECIAL CASE OF DIRECT MAIL

Recent studies of United States executives have shown that they value their direct mail when it contains relevant materials of specific interest to them, and that they read their mail carefully. Campaigns aimed at the top echelon of an organization demand and merit high quality and personalization in every way possible.

The widespread availability of computerized word-processing equipment with memory sufficient to store large mailing lists encourages the use of personalized methods in direct mail. Letters can be made to appear to be both original (in the old sense of custom preparation) and personalized (individually addressed and customized) because names and addresses can be fed directly into the letter in a seamless and inexpensive computer process. These letters are sent by first-class mail, and should always have the envelope prepared with a direct address (no labels). This type of program usually supports a sales person who follows up by telephone to get an appointment. The list is constructed from personally discovered qualified "leads" or is sent to an extremely well-qualified mailing list, and such lists do exist.

Private letter campaigns usually include a brochure, but because of the length and complexity of the most effective type of letter, it is not required. Long copy is used because it gives the initial impression that here is something to say that is worth reading; 1,500-word letters are not unusual in the United States, and the various formats for long letters that work well have become endowed with sales and marketing legend. Some direct mail experts speculate that the actual copy doesn't matter if the offer is good. Split response tests (trials where short and long versions of the same offer are sent to matched customers groups and the penetration rate for each is then compared for both letters) show that long copy sells more than short copy. There is some agreement that the headings and subheadings of the long letter should telegraph the benefits, but after that all is personal bias.

The primary benefit of the private letter campaign is that it makes the sales force more efficient. It can soften up the market, get the company product and salesperson known in his or her territory, be a lead generator, or be a customer qualification technique. It is expensive compared to a post-card campaign, but when its unit cost is compared to the cost of a sales call, it is very inexpensive.

CATEGORIES OF DIRECT MAIL

Some of the common categories of direct mail used for marketing and customer communications programs in the industry today are, in their increasing order of cost and importance: post-card programs; one-to-six page letter-sized flyer programs mailed in regular business envelopes; minibrochure programs of all types; omnibus brochure programs of all types; omnibus kit folder programs; computer disk demonstration programs; new product announcement kits complete with detailed use instructions and pricing information; and new user kits of all types, in many different formats (sometimes including printed user manuals and manual updates). All of these are sent by surface mail of the appropriate class for the audience.

EXAMPLES OF DIRECT MAIL

The selection below offers a rare opportunity to contrast and compare mailing pieces from different online vendors doing the same job with the same qualified buyers, at exactly the same point in the buying and sales cycle. They are all drawn from a single type of direct mail campaign, one aimed at prequalified hands-on initial buyers. The buyers are qualified by their purchase of a new computer system or a modem, or both, and their names and current addresses are obtained from the computer and modem vendors (in some cases, these pieces are included with the computer and/or modem vendor's own user and sales materials).

Their precision in reaching the market is the critical tactical point to be studied in these examples; they are zeroed in on qualified online customers by their timely use of the computer and modem buyer name and address list—since this list approaches 100 percent efficiency for online marketing purposes, every piece will reach a real potential buyer. If the piece is well designed and executed, and the offer and premiums are attractive and competitive, there is simply no more a direct mail program can do, except follow up well. If, however, the piece is sloppy or dull, or the offer is not competitive, a golden opportunity has been lost.

The mathematical elegance of this program is that the mailers close with the initial buyer at the very moment when his capability to use an online system has just been acquired: they play on and into the general excitement of the moment by raising the question of which online system to use and, if an online system has been chosen in advance of acquisition but not yet contracted, they try to reopen the issue by their offers. The sellers know full well that they are competing head-to-head for the sale and that a win in this battle will require all of the tricks in the direct mail book, and maybe some new inventions, too.

The examples show what is done when high-order efficient direct mail marketing tactics are used to the full in a marketing fire fight. If there is any occasion in direct mail worthy of our interest, it is this one. The work below should be the best work being done anywhere in this market because the stakes are as high as they can get in this segment of the market. In the course of the analysis the reader will be able to discern for himself the technical archetypes for

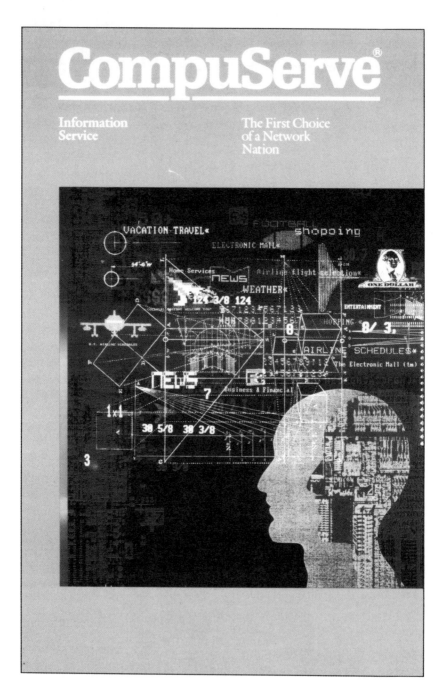

Figure 6.1. A mailing by CompuServe: side one.

most online marketing direct mailings in the United States, and one example from Great Britain will be a creative inspiration and challenge to all online marketers who target the hands-on initial buyer and use a fee-for-use pricing scheme. By studying the comparisons the reader will be able to judge the various marketing strategies and see how directly they affect both content and design.

CONTENT ANALYSIS

Side One. This is the "deluxe" approach centering on building an image for the service as one of the highest quality. The idea is conveyed through the exalted imagination of its imagery and its presentational format. The logo (name/signature/mark of the firm) is presented above the superb illustration depicting the information environment and the user in a sophisticated international graphic style. The total effect is that of a small-scale world-class poster, "suitable for framing."

Side Two. The panel shown above replaces a clever, visually elegant, customized panel entitled "All Booted Up and No Place to Phone." It was the perfect counterpart for the illustration. Its content called CompuServe the online connection to information and data services and especially to one's fellow *up-scale* PC users. Its appeal stressed that online participation in CompuServe is interactive and human at a high level of sophistication, and offered to satisfy the need that many accomplished and urbane users have for collegiality when working alone with the PC and an online system—a major benefit. Recently that approach has been replaced by the list of features shown above.

COMMENT The illustration on side one dramatizes the theme but fails to connect visually with side two, creating, in effect, two mailing pieces in one. Side two fails to reinforce the suggestion of powerful interaction with and mastery of the world at large through the PC. A coupon and offer are included. The coupon takes up 15 percent of the page space. (There is a discussion of coupons at the end of this section.)

CONTENT ANALYSIS

Side One. This is a "plain vanilla" approach that centers on the features of the service. Stylized symbols representing education, medicine, computers, money, news, and general interest topics are presented against a pink-tinted background. They are memory icons designed to aid the reader in learning the range of the major offerings. Claims are made about the comprehensive features of the databases, A to Z, etc. A detachable two-sided coupon is included. The coupon takes up 33 percent of the space of the piece.

Hundreds of thousands of personal computer owners who helped make CompuServe the largest online information service in North America got started with a complimentary subscription offer just like this.

No matter what kind of computer you have, the CompuServe Information Service will help you get the most out of it. CompuServe is an easy-to-learn and simple to use personal information service. It requires no special knowledge of computers or programming. Through a local call in most cities, almost any model of personal computer or terminal links you to over 700 online offerings for home, office, home-office or Home Office . . .

● **Personal Computing.** Join Forums that support leading microcomputer models and best-selling software.

● **Travel.** Check flight schedules and fares. Book flights. Compare accommodations and rates at hotels worldwide.

● **News, Weather & Sports.** Scan or "clip and save" articles you specify from the AP wires or The Washington Post.

● **Money Matters & Markets.** Retrieve market quotes. Study commodities contracts. Shop for mutual funds.

● **Entertainment & Games.** Play interactive adventure, space and war games; plus board or parlor games like casino blackjack, chess or trivia.

● **Financial Transaction Services.** Tap the convenience of electronic banking and broking for small businesses and homes.

● **Electronic Shopping.** Browse The Electronic MALL™ to comparison shop or purchase brand-name items in stores.

● **Home, Health & Family.** Consult medical or cooking texts. Comparison shop for new cars. Join special interest groups.

● **Education.** Compare programs of U.S. and Canadian colleges. Join educators from similar specialty areas.

● **Professionals Reference.** Search hundreds of national and international databases, indices and publications via online gateways.

● **Business and Other Interests.** Retrieve demographic data by city state or zip code. Meet with peers. Search a calendar of seminars by keyword.

● **Communications & Bulletin Boards.** Send electronic mail, including message exchange with Telex or MCI Mail. Contribute to bulletin boards or conferences.

Be a part...or be apart.

This introductory subscription contains. . .
● a private User ID number and password
● a $15.00 introductory usage credit
● a complimentary subscription to CompuServe's monthly newsmagazine, *Online Today*, once you subscribe.

Order yours from CompuServe directly with this coupon, or call:

800-848-8199
In Ohio, Call 1-614-457-0802

Name _____

Address _____

City _____

State _____ Zip _____

Phone _____

NOT REDEEMABLE

CompuServe ®

CompuServe Information Service
P.O. Box 20212
5000 Arlington Centre Blvd.
Columbus, Ohio 43220

An H&R Block Company

Figure 6.2. A mailing by CompuServe: side two.

BRING THE INFORMATION RESOURCES OF THE WORLD INTO YOUR HOME OR SCHOOL WITH KNOWLEDGE-INDEX℠

KNOWLEDGE INDEX is a powerful, low-cost information retrieval service which gives you access to a selected group of databases. These databases contain references and summaries of over 18 million articles, books, conference papers, technical reports, software packages and government documents. Virtually every subject is covered, from Accounting to Zoology.

KNOWLEDGE INDEX also offers you **DIALMAIL℠**, an electronic mail service that allows you to send messages, post announcements on bulletin boards, and join conferences with other users.

With **KNOWLEDGE INDEX** you can:

■ Locate software programs available for your microcomputer

■ Find reviews of movies, books, restaurants and consumer products

■ Keep up with the latest developments in your field, whether it's medicine or microelectronics

■ Introduce students to computer-based research techniques

■ Research college and university programs and requirements

FROM THE WORLD LEADER IN ONLINE DATABASES

KNOWLEDGE INDEX is a service of DIALOG* Information Services, Inc. DIALOG offers the world's leading online information retrieval service, used for over a decade by corporations, universities, libraries, and professionals.

*DIALOG is a registered servicemark, U.S. Patent & Trademark Office.

$ INTRODUCTORY OFFER $

Save $10 when you join **KNOWLEDGE INDEX** with the attached discount coupon. You pay only $25 for your one-time start-up fee plus 40¢ per minute connect time. You will receive **TWO FREE HOURS** of search time during your first 30 days of use, a self-instructional manual, and a quarterly **KNOWLEDGE INDEX** newsletter - and no monthly fee or minimum! To sign up, complete the attached discount coupon and return it to:

KNOWLEDGE INDEX
DIALOG Information Services, Inc.
3460 Hillview Avenue
Palo Alto, CA 94304
800-3-DIALOG

Online Mktg Strategies

Figure 6.3.   A mailing by KNOWLEDGE-INDEX: side one.

KNOWLEDGE-INDEX

KNOWLEDGE INDEX databases offer a broad spectrum of information sources. From the merely curious to the serious researcher, **KNOWLEDGE INDEX** has information for everyone.

 EDUCATION, including reading, special education, computer-assisted instruction, educational administration, and more are included in the ERIC database covering information from 1966 to the present. PETERSON'S COLLEGE DATABASE lists descriptions of colleges and universities, admissions information, financial aid information, a profile of students and more!

 MEDICINE & PSYCHOLOGY databases offer a complete range of information for these rapidly changing fields. MEDLINE, produced by the National Library of Medicine, covers current, worldwide developments in all phases of medicine, nursing and health care administration. DRUG INFORMATION FULLTEXT provides complete data and evaluation on more than 1,200 drugs. PSYCINFO and MENTAL HEALTH ABSTRACTS provide fast access to over 750,000 references on psychology and mental health.

 COMPUTER & ELECTRONIC information grows constantly in these fast-paced areas of interest. .MENU -- THE INTERNATIONAL SOFTWARE DATABASE lists more than 10,000 software programs and the MICROCOMPUTER INDEX covers 40 personal computer journals. Locate technical information and product reviews on computers, telecommunications, and electronics from the COMPUTER DATABASE. Worldwide engineering and physics literature from the ENGINEERING LITERATURE INDEX and INSPEC are also as close as your computer keyboard.

 BUSINESS INFORMATION provides valuable insight for investing, business opportunities, career path guidance, and a variety of other business topics. STANDARD & POOR'S CORPORATE DESCRIPTIONS and NEWS databases include account and balance sheet figures, stock and bond data, reports on consolidated earnings, and the latest mergers and acquisitions on over 7,800 publicly-held corporations. Through ABI/INFORM you also have access to articles from over 550 journals such as *Business Week*, *Forbes*, *Harvard Business Review*, and *Journal of Marketing*. TRADE & INDUSTRY INDEX covers manufacturing and industry literature.

 CURRENT AFFAIRS provides cover-to-cover indexing for *The New York Times*, *The Wall Street Journal*, *Christian Science Monitor*, *The Washington Post*, and *The Los Angeles Times* through the NEWSEARCH database.

 GENERAL INTEREST information from more than 400 popular journals such as *Time*, *Consumer Reports*, *Byte*, and *Money* are provided in the MAGAZINE INDEX. Over 25,000 government publications on topics such as agriculture, energy, housing, education, and nutrition are included in the GPO PUBLICATIONS REFERENCE database. And you can do basic research on any topic in the ACADEMIC AMERICAN ENCYCLOPEDIA online. Search detailed biographical information on outstanding professionals in all fields with MARQUIS WHO'S WHO and get assistance on your Federal Income Tax filing from the complete texts of 71 Internal Revenue Service publications with the IRS TAXINFO database.

Sign me up for a one-time start-up fee of $25 (REDUCED $10 FROM THE REGULAR $35 FEE), and bill the start-up and connect-time charges, including telecommunications, at the rate of 40¢ per minute to the credit card listed below.*

Charge my: ___ Visa ___ MasterCard ___ American Express

(Note: **KNOWLEDGE INDEX** is available **ONLY** through these credit cards. Direct monthly invoicing is available for libraries and academic institutions with enduser programs. Contact DIALOG Marketing for details.)

Account No. _____ Expiration Date: ___ / ___ / ___

Signature: _____

Name (please print): _____

Address: _____

City: _____ State: _____ Zip: _____

Telephone, day: (___) _____

Telephone, evening: (___) _____

*Send my **KNOWLEDGE INDEX** User's Workbook, password, and contract immediately. I understand that I must sign and return the **KNOWLEDGE INDEX** contract within 30 days to keep my password active.

Coupon offer expires December 31, 1987. Offer void where prohibited.

Online Mktg Strategies

Figure 6.4. A mailing by KNOWLEDGE-INDEX: side two.

Side Two. Each of the graphics is repeated at the head of a paragraph listing the features of the service. The intent is sober credibility for the service.

COMPARISON. CompuServe is positioned as a world-class, up-scale, consumer service with business and professional information available among its many choices. KNOWLEDGE-INDEX is positioned as a high-powered documentary no-nonsense service for business and the professions, with some other choices like DIALMAIL added on.

The difference in their positions is immediately apparent when these two pieces are compared closely. The up-scale appeal of the CompuServe piece will reach the high level segment in the consumer service and business/professional buyer market. The sober high credibility of the KNOWLEDGE-INDEX piece will reach, presumably, all the "serious" users of online services in all markets. The intensity of the CompuServe approach segregates the market by taste, income, and insight. KNOWLEDGE-INDEX wants to reach as many people as possible with its appeal, so the intensity is kept low to prevent segregation of the market by an overly strong appeal to one set of human interests or range of responses.

From this analysis we can observe several of the strengths of direct mail and see the marketing strategies that can be used to attract the audience and elicit their response. Note that benefits are conveyed to the reader by the mailer itself taken as a two-page whole. Neither of these mailers had to come out the way they did. It is not given anywhere that "plain vanilla" treatments will be sober or that "de-

Plain vanilla	Deluxe
KNOWLEDGE-INDEX	Compuserve
inexpensive production	expensive production
documentary look	quasi-documentary look
dense in features and fact	balanced in fact and features
large coupon	small coupon
not memorable	memorable
no emotional appeal to user	strong appeal to user's emotions
graceless (deliberately)	charming (deliberately)

Figure 6.5. Plain vanilla/deluxe comparison.

for those intent on
their own
pursuits.

NewsNet
$24 Free Introductory Time!
800-345-1301

Figure 6.6.   A mailing by NewsNet: side one.

luxe" treatments will be sweeping and exciting. The difference is in the creativity, clarity and taste of the marketing team as they build a response for their targeted audience model. (See the next two examples for a reversal of the use of production values.) Each of these schemes support the basic appeals being made to their buyer audience. They couldn't contrast more with each other if they tried deliberately to do so. The reader should note that this shows clearly the very wide range of expression possible in this class of market communications.

CONTENT ANALYSIS

Side One.   This is a well-produced communications and marketing enigma.

Side Two.   This presentation is, in total effect, a coupon, with an offer above it (the coupon uses about 25 percent of the total area but it dominates side two to the extent that the whole side seems to be a coupon). The price offer is good and it is presented forcefully.

CONTENT ANALYSIS

Side One.   This side presents a simple, unflattering cartoon of a nerd, to whom the question is addressed. He is shown in his starkly empty house using his first and only possession, his new computer.

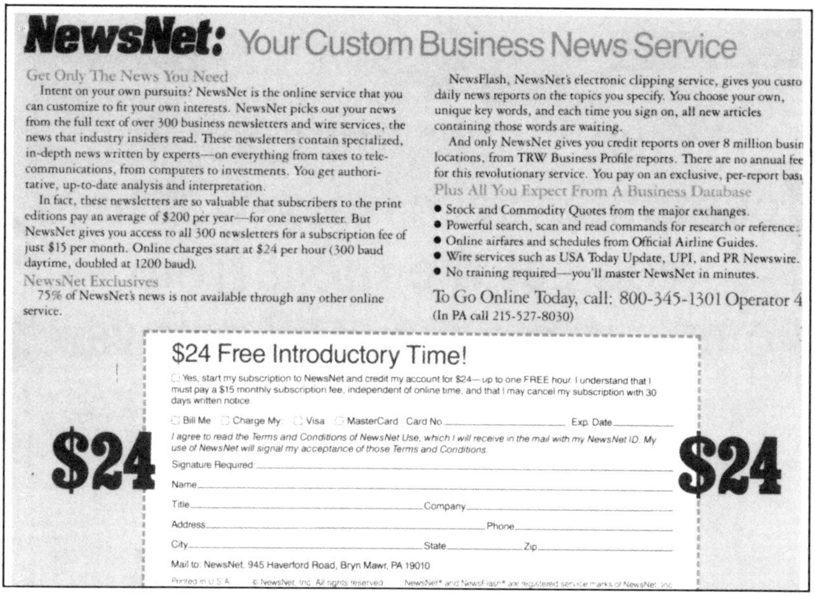

NewsNet: Your Custom Business News Service

Get Only The News You Need
Intent on your own pursuits? NewsNet is the online service that you can customize to fit your own interests. NewsNet picks out your news from the full text of over 300 business newsletters and wire services, the news that industry insiders read. These newsletters contain specialized, in-depth news written by experts—on everything from taxes to telecommunications, from computers to investments. You get authoritative, up-to-date analysis and interpretation.

In fact, these newsletters are so valuable that subscribers to the print editions pay an average of $200 per year—for one newsletter. But NewsNet gives you access to all 300 newsletters for a subscription fee of just $15 per month. Online charges start at $24 per hour (300 baud daytime, doubled at 1200 baud).

NewsNet Exclusives
75% of NewsNet's news is not available through any other online service.

NewsFlash, NewsNet's electronic clipping service, gives you custo daily news reports on the topics you specify. You choose your own, unique key words, and each time you sign on, all new articles containing those words are waiting.

And only NewsNet gives you credit reports on over 8 million busin locations, from TRW Business Profile reports. There are no annual fee for this revolutionary service. You pay on an exclusive, per-report basi

Plus All You Expect From A Business Database
- Stock and Commodity Quotes from the major exchanges.
- Powerful search, scan and read commands for research or reference:
- Online airfares and schedules from Official Airline Guides.
- Wire services such as USA Today Update, UPI, and PR Newswire.
- No training required—you'll master NewsNet in minutes.

To Go Online Today, call: 800-345-1301 Operator 4
(In PA call 215-527-8030)

$24 Free Introductory Time!

☐ Yes, start my subscription to NewsNet and credit my account for $24—up to one FREE hour. I understand that I must pay a $15 monthly subscription fee, independent of online time, and that I may cancel my subscription with 30 days written notice.

☐ Bill Me ☐ Charge My: ☐ Visa ☐ MasterCard Card No. _____ Exp. Date _____

I agree to read the Terms and Conditions of NewsNet Use, which I will receive in the mail with my NewsNet ID. My use of NewsNet will signal my acceptance of those Terms and Conditions.

Signature Required: _____

Name _____

Title _____ Company _____

Address _____ Phone _____

City _____ State _____ Zip _____

Mail to: NewsNet, 945 Haverford Road, Bryn Mawr, PA 19010

Printed in U.S.A.   © NewsNet, Inc. All rights reserved.   NewsNet® and NewsFlash® are registered service marks of NewsNet, Inc.

Figure 6.7. A mailing by NewsNet: side two.

Side Two. This side has the answer to the question posed on the other. The nerd's house is now full of the nerdy stuff he ordered from Comp-u-store. This is a very effective use of a forty-year-old technique, invented by Rosser Reeves, called the "optical cure." The problem and the cure are presented in a simple easy-to-comprehend visual situation and sequence that takes full advantage of the storytelling opportunity inherent in simply flipping over a sheet of paper. The appeal is to use Comp-u-store to gain a money-saving time and convenience advantage. A coupon is presented; it takes up about one fifth of page two.

THE TWO-TAILED COMP-U-STORE OFFER   Comp-u-store is careful to make a tandem offer in its copy that is quite as important as the online offer (it may even be more important), and has a great bearing on the positioning of the product. Membership in the service gets the subscriber a "free" Visa card but only "if you are credit qualified." This means that the appeal is targeted to the youngest tier of the market and explains much of the text. If the card can be issued, then the user can use Comp-u-store's services up to his credit limit. Don't forget that the list used for this mailing consisted of new computer and modem buyers, hence the image on the top of page one and the use of the credit appeal make a lot of sense, and may demonstrate empathy to some buyers. Two solid benefits are presented in the mailer.

What single, inexpensive computer accessory will help you get the most from your new modem and software?

Figure 6.8.   A mailing by Comp-u-store OnLine: side one. Comp-u-Store OnLine is a service of CUC International, Inc.

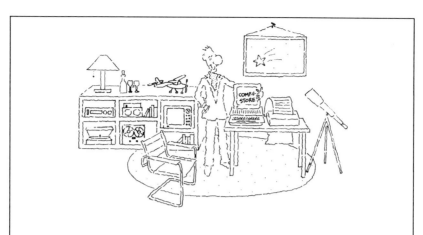

Comp-u-store OnLine.

Put your computer to work for you, saving money on everything you buy.

As a Comp-u-store OnLine member, you'll have access to our remarkable database of more than 250,000 name-brand products, all priced at huge discounts (10%-50% and more off manufacturers' suggested list prices!).

Shopping is fun and easy. While on Compu-Serve, type "GO CUS" and browse through listings of VCRs, stereos, cameras, home appliances, sports

equipment, whatever you're interested in. All at better-than-sale prices.

Purchases are delivered to your door in factory-sealed cartons with all warranties and guarantees in full effect.

One year's membership is only $25 plus CompuServes' minimal online connect time charges. Your savings will more than make up the membership fee with your very first purchase.

To join, type GO CUS while on CompuServe or complete and mail the coupon below.

Name _____

Address _____

City _____

State _____ Zip Code _____

Visa or MC # _____

Exp Date _____

Signature _____
I understand that I may cancel at any time during my first year of membership and receive a full $25 refund, no questions asked. Offer expires January 1, 1987.

Return to: **compⓤstore** OnLine 707 Summer Street
0; 90003; 0   Stamford, CT 06901

Figure 6.9.   A mailing by Comp-u-store OnLine: side two.

COMPARISON OF THE MEANS OF EXPRESSION "Deluxe" means are used by NewsNet to no specific marketing end in a disconnected two-sided presentation that undercuts an excellent price offer, and "plain vanilla" is used by Comp-u-store to solid advantage and with great skill in the adoption of television's optical cure technique to a print format that gets across quickly and memorably two important benefits.

COUPONS

The coupon is a low-budget salesman's call with his offer, his contract, and his "close" (asking for the business), all rolled into one. It must focus and restate the entire appeal in a single complex statement, show what will be delivered, when, and for how much. It must show the company name and address. It must be styled for the job it is trying to do, which is to steer the reader into becoming the right type of buyer. If the intention of the seller is to get the reader to buy by calling a toll free number, the coupon will still be present in most direct mail pieces (and advertisements), but it will be deliberately designed to be unuseable as a handwritten document compared to those coupons meant expressly to be sent in. (The benefits of the call to the seller are given below.)

This approach slightly contradicts one popular theory of direct mail, which holds that there is a special benefit to the seller in getting the buyer to send the coupon that isn't obtained when the buyer calls, namely, that the behavior exhibited in writing out the coupon and mailing it forms a higher level of commitment to the product. Behaviorally based commitments can be grown into brand loyalty. The amount of space given to the coupon is determined by the marketing plan and is a major cue for the reader to the behavior expected from him by the seller.

The CompuServe and Comp-u-store coupons seem to be designed to get the buyer to call in as the first (behavioral) choice and to send the coupon as the second (behavioral) choice. Using the toll-free number has the advantage of getting the account active with the benefits of immediate new revenue for the seller and an increase in the subscriber base.

CompuServe

The coupon uses one eighth of the space on side two, is very small, has to be cut out carefully with scissors (cutting ruins the illustration on the other side), and is designed in an almost unusable handwritten format. Also, the glossy printed surface is hard to write on. A prominent toll-free phone number is presented as the best alternative to the almost nonfunctional coupon.

The Comp-u-store, Knowledge-Index, and NewsNet coupons seem to be designed to get the reader to send the card in, thereby obtaining for the seller the behavioral advantage inherent in this type of transaction:

Comp-u-store

The coupon uses one fifth of the space on side two, is in a square format, and is almost unusable as a handwritten document format. There is no toll-free number.

Knowledge-Index

The coupon uses one third of the space on both sides of the piece, and looks like a typical grocery or retail discount coupon. This is a serious coupon with a perforation across the top to allow it to be torn off readily and then mailed in an envelope. It would be hard to write on and even harder to read when it is received by the seller. There is no toll-free number.

NewsNet

The coupon uses one fourth of the space on side two, is a functional handwritten document format, and stresses the price appeal right on the edges of the coupon. It is designed to be cut out and mailed in an envelope. A toll-free number is given above the coupon, but the coupon is the main show.

Introduction

In figures 6.10 and 6.11, InfoLine's mailer is shown completely unfolded, a condition that makes it appear as two confusing continuous images. For purposes of analysis, the images have been divided into four "panels." In the text that follows, the panels are examined in their presentational order as seen by the reader. The "P-numbers" indicate the panel being mentioned.

Try to imagine the piece first as folded and then being slowly unfolded by the reader. A study of the unfolding sequence is important because the act of unfolding is an integral part of the interest of this mailing piece.

A Summary of the Unfolding Operations:

(cover) = (½ of panel one) + (½ of panel two)
panel one, when opened, reveals → (all of panel two) + (⅙th of panel three)

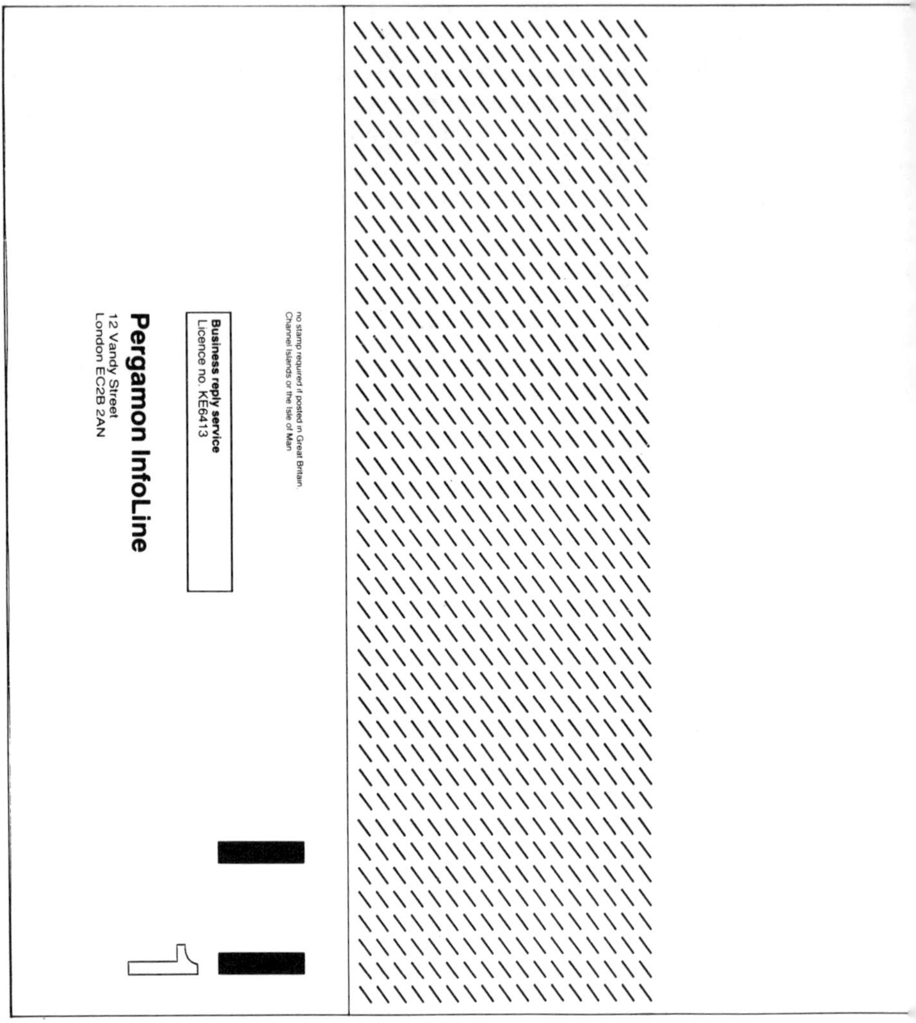
no stamp required if posted in Great Britain, Channel Islands or the Isle of Man
Business reply service
Licence no. KE6413
Pergamon InfoLine
12 Vandy Street
London EC2B 2AN

(P_2)

Figure 6.10. A mailing piece by InfoLine: side A.

panel two, when opened, reveals → (all of panel three and an actual search card)
panel four = back cover

(P_1). THE FOLDED STATE: THE COVER IS COMPOSED OF 1/2 OF PANEL ONE AND 1/2 OF PANEL TWO The cover is two panels folded over each other. It opens from near its center. Panel one is the left hand portion. The background color is black, with a pattern of red colored strokes, each running diagonally from north

ERGAMON INFOLINE
12 Vandy Street
London EC2A 2DE
elephone: 01-377 4650
Telex: 8814614

A Division of
Pergamon Orbit InfoLine
Limited.

(P₄)   (P₁)

west to south east. An image of a "charge" card is positioned at a
contradictory angle. Using die cutting to shape the edge of the panel,
the image of the card has been made to tip out, overlapping panel
two.

The reader is meant to identify and appreciate the value implicit
in any charge card. No campaign theme is mentioned or shown, nor
does the InfoLine logo appear anywhere except on the image of the
card. The reader must turn the page to find the meaning "behind"
the image of the card. To do so, he will very likely handle the pro-

truding edge of the card. The image of the card foreshadows an actual card inside the mailer. Touching it is a form of behavioral "encouragement."

(P_2). THE HALF-OPENED STATE: PANEL ONE, WHEN OPENED, REVEALS ALL OF PANEL TWO AND 1/6 OF PANEL THREE   Panel two is the right-hand half of the cover. It is divided equally into two fields, the back of a preprinted postal return card on the left and a sector of red strokes against black. The two fields can't be designed to match visually because the address side of any paid return card is designed exactly to the specifications of the postal system.

Copy

There is no copy on panel two.

When panel one is opened, its underside is automatically exposed to the reader: the left-hand side of panel three is printed on the back of panel one, and, therefore, comes into view when it is opened. The actual search card is still covered by panel two.

The portion of panel three, now revealed on the left, has a full-color image of a man's face, with part of a screen from an online search printed nearby in reverse type. This particular area is the obverse of the die-cut card on the cover, so it has an irregular attention-getting shape.

The copy *above* the image now comes into play for the reader. Under the heading *Introduction*, an appeal to the user stresses the power of information in gaining competitive edge. InfoLine is then named and a major claim for leadership in the electronic information industry is made. *Below the image* are two additional headings, *Flexible* and *Up to date*, both of which list general features of the online system.

(P_3). THE FULLY OPENED STATE: PANEL TWO, WHEN OPENED, REVEALS ALL OF PANEL THREE AND AN ACTUAL SEARCH CARD   This panel contains the plastic search card itself, the reason for the mailing. Mounted in an easily detachable manner, the card is scaled like other charge cards, suitable for one's wallet. Unfortunately, in this version of the mailer, the card is introduced to the reader before any campaign theme has been established, an invitation to accept and use it has been given, or an adequate explanation of what kind of benefit or obligation is entailed in using or even having the card.

Copy

Above the illustration and card area, the copy continues, progressing to the right in two columns: at the end of a list of features in the third column comes the offer of an immediate online demonstration. Below the illustration, three more copy headings are presented, including the critical *Getting started* directions, at the far right.

Instructions

To the right of the illustration, at the top of the panel, under the heading *Instructions*, the modem and software settings, "dial-up," and "log on" details are listed in a single vertical column, all of which are necessary for access to InfoLine's database, and, most important, to enacting the behavioral cycle. The behavioral potential of the presentation and offer is next to worthless if they are confusing or hard to follow.

Return Card

On the far right is the detachable "paid postage return" or "business reply service" return card, designed to be mailed to InfoLine. It uses ½ of the total space of panel three and is a serious return card meant to be "redeemed" in exchange for the free search time. The copy on the card is confusing however, making the reader wonder if the offer of a free demonstration is valid before the return mail card is sent to InfoLine.

Comments

The combination of the two behavioral commitments on the part of the prospect—keeping the search card and mailing the return card—use the power of well-executed direct mail to get quick, but, one hopes, lasting commitments from the recipient.

Summary of the Behavioral Responses Sought from the Reader:

- Open the envelope (not shown here).
- Unfold the piece, read it, and find the card.
- Take the card out. Handle it.
- Accept the offer of a free demonstration in exchange for giving one's name to InfoLine.
- Set up the terminal, modem, and software to InfoLine's specifications.
- Go online and search successfully, thereby building the desire for more electronic information service.
- Send in the mail reply card to initiate the sales cycle.
- Accept and heed follow-up calls and mailings.
- Keep the Search Card and feel like a member of the InfoLine "club."
- Show and lend the card to others.

and, through the self-initiated activities above, to

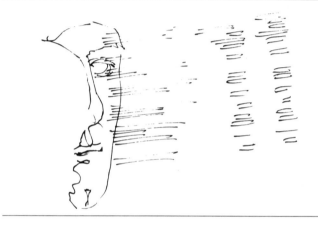

Introduction

The ability to make the right decision at the right time depends on many factors. But no matter how strong your powers of intuition, the power of accurate information is even stronger. Don't leave your decision making to chance – Pergamon InfoLine can give you the power you need to make well advised business decisions.

Pergamon InfoLine has been established in the business of online information for over ten years. During this time we have become a world leader in the provision of scientific, technical and patent information.

As part of our continual programme of expansion, Pergamon InfoLine identified vital need for business information. In the time since we entered this dynamic field, have built up an impressive portfolio of products to meet management needs. Ou databases come from well respected information providers such as Dun and Bradstreet, Jordan & Sons, BIS Infomat a many others.

Today Pergamon InfoLine offers you imme access to a comprehensive range of bus databases covering a wide variety of bus activities, including the facts on:

PERGAMON

SE
CA
USERN
BUSI

FLEXIBLE
Using InfoLine, you can target key companies by geographical, market or financial criteria and pinpoint the exact information you need in seconds using simple key words.

UP TO DATE
Most of our databases are updated weekly or monthly, ensuring a level of timeliness and accuracy unparallelled in hard copy directories.

CONVENIENT
This wealth of information is instantly acce from the convenience of your own office, u a micro-computer, modem and telephone dial into our computer.

COST EFFECTIVE
Why pay for a whole library of information you only need selected items? Using InfoL you only pay for the information you actually There is no subscription fee or up-front cha

(P₃)

Figure 6.11. A mailing piece by InfoLine: side B.

- Learn InfoLine's name and gain a favorable impression of the company and the service.
- Learn about online information services and think well of them.
- Get an actual payoff from the demonstration.
- Develop a commitment to becoming and remaining a user of the service, and to pay for those services.
- Advocate and "resell" InfoLine in the buying organization.

ll UK registered companies
40,000 credit ratings and UK
ompany accounts
lmost half a million marketing
rofiles
very major retail outlet in Britain
40,000 British manufacturing and
istribution locations
ummaries from over 1000
orldwide newspapers and journals
ll UK trade marks and patents
00,000 international corporate
tructures

SEARCHCARD will give you immediate
ss to a free demonstration of our services
:an be used as many times as you like.

ou can choose in which format you wish to
ve the information.

TING STARTED

ly follow the instructions overleaf to use the
lemonstration and discover just how
ble to your company InfoLine will be.

need advice on equipment, or would like
information about our business databases,
y return the reply-paid card and we will
you details of our free introductory search
offer.

Instructions

To access InfoLine today simply set your
terminal and modem to the settings shown
and follow the dial-up and log-on procedures.
We will then be able to show you how valuable
InfoLine will be to you.

1. **Terminal Settings**

   Set your equipment to:
   Teletype/ASCII compatible Asynchronous
   mode

Full duplex	or	Full duplex
1 Start Bit		1 Start Bit
8 Data Bits		7 Data Bits
1 Stop Bit		1 Parity Bit*
No Parity		1 Stop Bit
		*parity disabled

   InfoLine operates at three speeds:
   Set your terminal and modem to:
   300 baud
   1200 baud
   1200/75 baud

2. **Dial-up**

   Dial the appropriate telephone number for
   your speed setting.
   300 baud   01 247 5446
   1200 baud   01 247 7621
   1200/75 baud   01 377 5050

   Pergamon InfoLine is also available
   through PSS. If you are already a
   subscriber to PSS you may access via
   either of our PSS addresses:

   A219200190
   A219201281

3. **Log-on**

   When the data connection is established
   press carriage return until you see the
   message.
   **WELCOME TO PERGAMON INFOLINE
   USERNAME:**
   Type in the Username on the enclosed
   SearchCard i.e.
             BUSINESS
   to access our demonstration.
   Telephone our **Help Desk on 01-377 4957** if
   you need any help.
   For immediate registration or more detailed
   information, complete and return the pre-paid
   card attached.

Please send me documents for immediate registration
Please send me detailed information on
Business Information files
Science and Technology files
Patent and Trademark files
Please contact me to arrange a full demonstration.

Position
Telex
Name
Organisation
Address
Telephone

Dominance

About ¼ of the total presentation area is used to deliver the two cards
to the user, which conveys their importance to the reader. The actual
presence of a usable "charge" card is also an attention getting device.

Pricing

No barrier is placed in between the customer and system use. Instead,
the door is opened. These combined marketing tactics suit the pricing

Figure 6.12.   A user card by InfoLine.

scheme of the service perfectly: no front-end fees are charged by InfoLine, but user fees are charged on each use occasion. Free use starts the buyer off in the right manner by building a pattern of quick acceptance and use.

Printing and Design

Unlike the other panels, uneven printing reproduction mars the quality of panel three: the full-color illustration is sour and brownish, the type is mushy, the black-red-brown-green-white color scheme is particularly discordant and unresolved. The graphic design of panel three fails to highlight or dramatize the card itself, one of the key features of InfoLine's earlier efforts. The appearance of the card itself is uneven and strident in this context. The combined effects of design choices and printing techniques yield a confusing visual communications structure for panel three.

(P_4.) BACK COVER   This panel is isolated from the overall appeal by the mechanical folding of the mailer. It presents only the address of the firm.

Analysis of the Search Card

Possessing the card gives a sense of membership and authority. The value to InfoLine is slightly undercut in this version of the Search Card. Although expensive to produce, it looks and feels cheap. Earlier cards in this series were handsome productions, and the execution was of high quality. Still, the card shown here speaks pretty well for InfoLine at most levels of communication. The unusual plastic stock, tactile qualities, trimming, and color scheme differentiate it from the other credit and ID cards the reader might carry.

Conclusion

In marketing terms, this sophisticated direct mail project gets the prospect working with and thinking about InfoLine in a prompt, direct, and personal way. It meets the test of using the power of direct mail to superior advantage. The behavioral aspects surrounding the card and the offer it conveys are very well thought through and compellingly organized. The issue of customer continuity is handled in one gulp, and the quality of the service itself is left to be its own best spokesperson.

At the level of production and presentation detail, this version of the mailer and card has some shortcomings not present in the earlier versions. Particularly striking is the absence of a specific campaign theme connecting the mailer to the ongoing advertising and public relations programs of the firm. While this approach enhances the shelf life of an expensive direct mail piece, it ignores the benefits of the combined effects of all three influences on the individual buyer's behavior and the market as a whole.

6.3. Direct Telemarketing

Consider the advantages to an online marketing organization from investing in and perfecting the use of telemarketing.

The third tool that is underutilized by many online organizations is direct telemarketing. While most online organizations have customer service functions (usually reached by toll-free numbers) for supporting the customer in his searching activities and for helping him cope with arcane communications like billing and user manuals, these services respond to the customer's call for help. In direct telemarketing programs the company calls the prospect or customer for the purpose of selling. (Customer support services fall outside the marketing purpose of direct telemarketing and are not covered in this book.)

Telemarketing saves money because it is "time and territory" efficient at a low cost. In the rank order of all selling costs, telemarketing falls near the low end of the scale. As a method of selling it is efficient, making many more customer contacts per telemarketing salesperson day than a field sales force can possibly make in a day. Telemarketing sales-force staff costs are lower than direct sales-force staff costs because good telemarketers can be drawn from the pool of inexperienced sales talent and are therefore lower paid.

Marketing managers say that the success of selling through telemarketing is dependent on the nature of pricing. If the deal is priced as a large one-time-only initial commitment at sign-up, telemarketing will be unsuccessful. It is successful in building use during the contract period, and can be used effectively in obtaining long-term contract renewals. If the deal requires a low initial commitment, telemarketing does well on the initial sale, but will have fewer successes in encouraging system use if the charge for use is high. A mine field that both direct mail and telemarketing have to cross is making the wrong sale when the initial sign-up fee for the service is low. When revenue is generated by use of the system, one must plan carefully to assure that telemarketing tactics do not result in a large number of nominal "users" who never use the system.

MARKETING AIMS

A telemarketing function can fulfill many marketing aims. The first task in a telemarketing program is to define them. The following six points should be considered.

- Test the receptivity of new markets and find sales leads. All too often in online marketing programs not enough is known about the target market. Who owns and uses computers in a given market can be hard to find out. Even harder is to find the modem-equipped systems. In addition to these unknowns, there are ambiguities about who will be the hands-on user of the system and who will be the enduser of information, and so on. If an online organization is attempting to crack a new market, and it has a prospect list that is not deemed strong or has a list of major organizations it wants to crack, telemarketing can be an easy way to test the receptivity of the new market, as well as a way to identify who the decision makers and users will be. Another important telemarketing function in new markets is to generate and qualify buyer leads using the same methods as those for testing receptivity but adopting what was learned from the market research phase as the structure of the leads program.

- Soften up the market for direct sales calls. A direct sales person can spend a lot of time just walking around in a market before he or she can actually identify buyers or users. Telemarketing can bring wandering to a standstill by identifying the interested buyers and users.
- Close initial sales. A proper and binding initial commitment is the determinant of success in initial sales by phone because many phone orders never materialize if these first steps aren't taken properly. Telemarketing can close sales over the phone if the service can be paid by credit card because all of the account-opening red tape can be completed during the call. In institutional sales, a complete follow-up program is required because the buyer usually needs a purchase order with appropriate signatures and wants to be billed directly. (If institutional sales are undertaken by telemarketing, it is critical that sales incentives owed to telemarketers not be paid until a signed contract is in hand.)
- Capture market share from another vendor. To increase share by counterselling tactics is a natural program for telemarketing. The buyers are already online service users, they know how systems operate (and malfunction) and what the benefits are, and they usually have a rough idea of their charges. The telemarketing task is to describe vividly the comparative advantages of the seller's system versus that of the competitors and to close the sale. Telemarketers must master pricing and charges on both systems and be able to speak to the differences. This kind of selling eliminates several expensive and risky steps for the seller and uses the buyer's knowledge of online systems to the seller's advantage.
- Find new users. The strongest marketing tactic in the online business is a customer referral by a happy user. Telemarketing can be successful in finding new users in an organization that already has some satisfied customers. This program works best in large complex buyer organizations. Telemarketing begins by talking to users, and by getting referrals to other departments and people who may have an interest. It keeps using this program over and over to maximize penetration within the buyer organization. (Caution: if the satisfied users are in the library or the information service of a major organization, they may be reluctant to refer the seller to the libraries' customers.) This program is most successful when selling to endusers of information, but they can be hard to locate and get on the phone.
- Build use among current customers. This revenue building tactic is the most underutilized in the online industry. Call topics can range from those designed simply to keep the service's

name in the front of the user to fully developed use-building presentations complete with sample searches of the proper type for that user. The programs vary with the type of user; for example, if the user is a librarian, the aim is to redirect use from other online systems to one's own; if the user is an end-user, probably the user has an online system, so his use of that system is discussed, and so on. The seller must ensure that the user remembers that he or she has the seller's online service and knows how useful it is in the user's everyday activities. Sales pitches work best if both the user and the seller can be "online" and "on phone" at the same time. This often produces a logistical conflict since the user must have two phone lines available and have the "voice" phone within reach of the computer. Telemarketing should never be undertaken by a staff member who is not expert in the use of the system, and telemarketers must have access to the system while they are on the phone with the client. (Computerized telemarketing equipment is perfect for online organizations, and the investment can be amortized quickly by those systems with the right type of pricing.)

A marketing campaign has many pieces, ranging from attendance at international tradeshows and worldwide advertising, at one extreme, to a post card mailed to the current users in one organization followed by a phone call to each of them from direct telemarketing, at the other. Scope comes out of corporate style, market, product, and revenue potential. Both large and small campaigns require careful planning and coordination in all their details and nuances, and tight management of their expenses.

The mix of marketing tools to be used in a campaign has to be well chosen. Part of the choice is determined by market research. Market research supporting direct mail and telemarketing is, when used together in a well-planned, coordinated, and executed campaign, a powerful program mix. It may seem obvious to the reader that one cannot go out and dump thousands of pieces of direct mail into the postal box, each of which asks buyers to respond by using a toll-free number, when only one person is available at one phone to take buyers' responses, but it happens with discouraging frequency.

The organization's marketing goals must be very clear when determining how sales people are paid for their sales. Most organizations have an incentive plan for sales people, including their telemarketers. In a new market it makes sense for the incentive to be tied to the capture of new customers. If, however, pricing generates revenue from use, an incentive plan that gives rewards for new customers can mean that the incentive plan is paying for "above plan" performance (i.e., more new customers than expected) while the organization's revenue goal is below "plan" (i.e., use is lower than expected). This can be very difficult to explain to senior management or a board of directors. This situation may be entirely appropriate; however, it must be understood and agreed to at the highest levels of the organization. Both pricing and sales incentives policy in the online industry must be weighed carefully. Sales incentives must be in line with market realities.

6.4. Public Relations in Support of Marketing Programs

Consider the many advantages to an online marketing organization from investing in and perfecting the use of public relations.

Few online organizations have public relations programs supporting marketing, or the organization as a whole. It is not an overstatement to say that public relations can play a productive role in all of the company's audiences and markets, simultaneously and continuously. Of special interest is the ability of public relations programs to be harnessed to specific marketing opportunities at the time when they are current and important to the success of the marketing program.

Ironically, public relations has an image problem in the online industry. It, and market research, are often viewed as high-altitude stuff, far above sea level. Like market research, it has its detractors, the manager/technocrat/self-proclaimed pragmatist triad who can't see much payoff, if any. The triad is joined by some marketers who judge the cost/benefit ratio of public relations programs as inadequate because its benefits are seen as unmeasurable.

All of these critics ignore the evidence that the tide in high tech marketing is running in favor of more market research and public relations. The trend is based on the success they have brought to marketing. Public relations counselors such as Regis McKenna, in his work for Apple Computers, and A. E. "Jeff" Jeffcoat, in his work for Mead Data Central, have shown that public relations programs work in high tech, that they have marketing and market relevance, and that public relations is a solid tool for supporting marketing programs.

PUBLIC RELATIONS ACTIVITIES IN SUPPORT OF MARKETING PROGRAMS

Public relations is one of the arms of marketing communications, working to increase marketing efficiency by favorably influencing buyer behaviors and the opinions of both buyers and others—in short, improving market efficiency at the buyer end. Public relations structures product and service communications in the market itself and creates relevant communications and events in the target markets to publicize and help accomplish marketing goals. Programs sometimes need to work through the press and other public forms of communication such as radio and television. Public relations practitioners are experts at getting and keeping the interest of journalists and other communicators, and through them reaching their audiences.

One way to think of public relations is as a truthful and timely communications process. It uses truthful communications tactics for getting others to speak and think well of the present and future of the companies' policies, marketing, products, services, and personnel. Unexpectedly, public relations programs produce results both internally and externally. In the process of developing a public relations case for the companies' products and services, marketing organizations learn about themselves as they are seen through the eyes of others. Gray areas in product and service programs come to light. Management difficulties are unearthed by the analysis that precedes public communications in support of marketing. In this sense, the in-house benefits are large indeed. Public relations in support of marketing is not a form of management consulting, nor should it be applied as such, but the spillover from its applications to marketing problems can have a good effect on marketing management, practice, and policy.

Imagine the value to the marketing effort of having a major article about the company and its products appear in the *Wall Street Journal*. A few years ago 97 percent of the total daily content of the *Wall Street Journal* was said to be comprised of stories based on press releases and press relations efforts by companies and organizations. This phenomenon is widespread; other papers like the *Financial Times* and the *Neue Zürcher Zeitung*, for example, also use this kind of material. In this sense public relations is an extension, so to speak, of the working press, finding and developing stories that the press would miss without the help of public relations to bring them to its attention. The percentage above demonstrates the volume of corporate news and underlines the competitive importance of corporate public relations at its simplest level—the preparation and timely release of accurate and useful "news" to the press.

Public relations practitioners are often former journalists who know the process of news gathering and who are fair judges of what is marketing and business news, and what isn't. In exercising their judgment they can make sure that the news provided to the press is given and received properly. The wisdom of this is shown in fairer and more frequent coverage of the companies' corporate and marketing issues, products, and personnel. Press coverage in and of itself (measured in tens of thousands of column inches) is rarely a goal in public relations; the aim is obtaining and managing the conditions that lead to obtaining the right coverage at the right time, in a reliable and impartial manner.

Public relations concentrates on the key audiences to be reached by the communication mission at hand. Sometimes those will be the audiences that are interested in and influenced by top management and company-wide actions and plans. When public relations is used in this manner it projects what the company is, and structures how it is perceived and appreciated. When used well, it reveals, sharpens, and enhances understanding of the organization's collective mystique, world view, personality, style, power, and achievements. It succeeds in making the truth about the company known by presenting it in a relevant and cogent style. In this sense it indirectly shapes and supports all of the other image-building activities of the organization including those that occur in marketing programs. Sometimes these functions are separated into corporate public relations programs that take on aims much wider than marketing.

Public relations manages timely streams of marketing information featuring those people, events, and developments in the whole organization that meet the test of being "news" in the public relations sense of the word. In the long run the image benefit gained from this approach is one of reliability and forthrightness in the organization's corporate culture, expressed publicly as trust in and concern for the audience's right, need, and ability to understand (and value) the achievements (and difficulties) of great enterprises. Public relations programs follow two roads when they enter this territory. One leads to the infrastructure of the online industry and the corps of industry watchers in paper publishing, finance, academia, the trade press, R & D, and so on; the other leads to the markets of the company. All roads lead to Rome however. By addressing the infrastructure directly and informing them on the company, products, and services, the information and advice the infrastructure gives to the market are more positive. By influencing the market, the market in its turn is more likely to give positive feedback on online products and services to the industry watchers in the infrastructure.

Most online organizations are small businesses of relative simplicity, easily understood by most of their audiences even when they are leaders in their segment of the electronic publishing industry. A public relations program is useful in supporting and reinforcing a single memorable image of the organization. In service organizations like those in the online industry, where the product is not tangible, a human face needs to be put on corporate and high-level marketing communications. This role is often filled by the CEO of the organization. Public relations can productively direct and manage the role of the CEO as a public spokesperson for the organization, a program that can be of great help in getting both corporate and marketing goals across to the organization's audiences and markets. This is even more important when the company is a market leader in the industry, because its management will often be called on to speak for the whole industry on local, national, or international industry issues.

A public relations program tailored to business relations is strongly indicated if the online organization cuts a poor figure in the industry, as judged by its technical peers and competitors, with its publishers or suppliers, or in the research and development community. The importance of the business and industry audience is in their power to make and influence opinion as often-consulted sources of information and ideas about the company and the industry. Their comments circulate widely among influential buyers and the trade and popular press. A public relations program can work at assuring that, ideally, all of these interested communities are neutrally disposed (at the very least) or enthusiastic (at best) about the company, its management, staff, pricing, services, products, markets, and future prospects. Public relations is the information arm of marketing for informing and softening up these critical audiences.

PUBLIC RELATIONS FUNCTIONS

Public relations activities are hard to talk about in a general sense. The tools and activities are situation sensitive and very flexible, as they must be to serve well the many complex situations that arise in human affairs. Public relations opportunities have to be analyzed from the ground up, and the tools chosen to fit the occasion. No other method will serve in public relations because there are no canned packages, programs, or formulas that suit all cases.

Increasing awareness and acceptance in both the Buyer and the Market

Buyer and market awareness and acceptance depends on achieving immediate recognition of the company's name and product/service images. Public relations in support of marketing puts out detailed information and indirect marketing communications about the company and its products and services, and, often, supportive information about the industry where that will be influential. The marketing assumption that a well-informed buyer is easier to sell and keep as a client, and that a well-informed government and public is no threat to the industry as a whole, is addressed directly by this kind of program.

The Translation Function

Explaining difficult-to-grasp technicalities that, when well understood by the market and public, will positively influence the market and be helpful in sales is another market related assignment for public relations. This is a translation function, changing the "difficult and abstract" into the "simple." New knowledge products combined with computer-based management programs are an example of marketing situations where this approach may be needed. It can also be used to explain the principle of online searching. (It is not, however, a useful technique for addressing cyberphobia among buyers and users.)

Featuring Specific Products and Services

On some marketing occasions, like the introduction of new products or services, specific people, buyers, markets, products, and services need to be featured individually within the framework of the marketing program. Public relations programs of this kind may draw on these and other hands-on activities.

- Building (a) interest in the specific subject in appropriate audiences; (b) traffic at company and industry sponsored events for all interested parties; (c) company and product images; and (d) name recognition in the market, community, nation, and world (if necessary).
- Publicizing (a) the people in the organization who make news; (b) the products and their applied benefits; and (c) the company and the industry as needed.
- Managing (a) press relations with the local, national, and international trade and press publications; (b) business and industry relations programs; (c) government relations; (d) marketing events; and (e) public affairs programs at all levels.

Creating Attention-getting and Significant Community, National, or International Events that Feature Prominent Individuals Not Associated with the Company

On some occasions the company will mount and sponsor specific meetings and events. Many of these events will merit prominent spokespersons. Company spokespersons are very important of course, but well-known spokespersons are often featured in these programs because they are credible to the audience (they have no real stake in the issues they speak to), attract the respect of the audience, and get the attention of the press. Professors, professionals, businessmen, community leaders, and commentators of all kinds can be persuaded to speak or be identified with product- or service-sponsored events. Programs of this kind are usually handled by public relations experts.

Managing Secondary Public Relations Programs

Companies often find it desirable to have their staff and management serve in leadership positions in key scientific and industry organizations. Secondary public relations is the art of securing these appointments, many of which are of indirect importance to the marketing program. These programs may involve a series of behind-the-scenes activities to get the appointment.

SUMMARY OF THE HANDS-ON ACTIVITIES OFTEN USED IN PUBLIC RELATIONS PROGRAMS

BUILDING   (a) interest in the company and the industry in appropriate audiences; (b) traffic at company- and industry-sponsored events for buyers and other interested parties; (c) use among all current customers; the total volume of use in a segment of the market and the total volume of use in the whole market; (d) company and product images; and (e) name recognition in the market, community, nation, and world (if necessary).

PUBLICIZING   (a) the people in the organization who make news; (b) the products and their applied benefits; and (c) the company and the industry as needed.

MANAGING   (a) press relations with local, national, and international trade and press publications; (b) business and industry relations programs; (c) government relations; (d) marketing events; and (e) public affairs programs at all levels.

CREATIVELY SUPPORTING   all other marketing communications and market research programs.

CREATING   marketing communications programs (where necessary) and sales support communications for sales forces.

INTRODUCING   (a) product images for new products and changing technologies; (b) new prospects to the service and the industry; (c) new markets to the company; (d) the press to the industry, the company, its products, services, and people; and (e) the company to the press and other interested local, national, and international corporate, market, and public individuals and audiences.

CORPORATE PUBLIC RELATIONS AIMS SOMETIMES HAVE A BEARING ON MARKETING GOALS

Public relations in support of marketing is often assigned marketing related corporate missions that, like corporate advertising, support the whole sphere of interest of the corporation but can seem to be far from the arena of the market. In one sense these missions are peripheral to the marketer's interests. On the other hand, corporate issues of all kinds are having more influence than ever on marketing in the topsy-turvy world of multinational mergers and divestitures.

7

CONCLUSION

I think that marketing must become a respected and influential peer of technology, product development, and management if the industry hopes to achieve its full potential. It would probably be better all round if marketing were first among equals. Few would disagree that marketing is playing a larger offensive and defensive role in the market successes of high tech companies. As high tech products proliferate, as markets change, and as industries mature, the greater the responsibility of marketing is to proactively sort out, manage, and use successfully all market opportunities. Also, any activity that builds solid relationships with the buyer, defends the companies' products and services from inroads by the competition and is sensitive in meeting the buyers' information and data needs, is an asset of real value in an increasingly competitive and mature market.

The online industry exploits a shrewd marriage of off-the-shelf data and off-the-shelf technology. It is hard to understand and credit the policy-making position given to technologists in the online industry. It has never been driven by a technological breakthrough; the "breakthrough" achieved by electronic publishing has been social and economic—upgrading, upsetting, and remaking the patterns and cost/benefit ratios of manual research, a market success.

While there may well be technological breakthroughs that could remake the online industry, the research and development required are out of reach and unjustified by the online markets developed so far. Even currently available technology is used passively and unimaginatively. Given all of this, how does the spell cast by technology continue to hypnotize one online organization after another? Marketers privately and bitterly complain of being shut out, while technocrats, mainly uninformed about the critical details of markets and customers, make the strategic decisions by shopping the electronic bazaar.

Marketing, not technology, should run the early warning radar of the company, scanning the marketing horizon for market data and competitive threats. It is charged with the corporate responsibility of keeping the company, its technology, products, services, image, etc., in tune with the changes and preferences of the market. The alternative, using technology to remake and increase the market, is proving to be a questionable wager not only in online markets but in high tech markets everywhere.

Davidow cites instances at Intel in which marketing saved threatened product lines by listening to the customer. The gain for Intel wasn't just in market share and new revenue; it also paid off in increased respect and improved corporate image that was then exploited to further their market position. In technologies like online systems, where buyer information and preferences can easily be fed back into service and product design for technical planning, technology should follow and react to marketing data that will increase the company's sales. Responding adequately to the needs of the customer has been done poorly in the online industry with the result that online services and online organizations remain too technically self-centered and indifferent.

ON-AGAIN, OFF-AGAIN MARKETING

High tech management is relearning old lessons like the uses for traditional beauty pageant marketing and how to create exciting product and service positioning concepts. There is growing lip service among online managements to the "old," easily discounted, issues of cyberphobic attitudes and reactions in the buyer. Also, online management is slowly coming to see that expert positioning and needs-gap recognition programs are one of the ways of devising thoughtful customer-sensitive products and crystal-clear marketing communications. These recognitions set the stage for better marketing and sales support programs in the online industry.

Marketing has been spotty and underfinanced in the online industry because its uneven performance has not been able to keep management's trust. Marketing has been used mainly to oil the technology/motivation cycle. Marketing used just as an oil can for technology looks "fuzzy," "high altitude," and expensively luxurious. No one points out forcefully enough that marketing too has a strong body of knowledge supporting it as a profession, a good track record in high tech, and a wide range of creative and analytical tools that it can apply either quickly or over time to both short-lived and long-term market problems. If the full weight of marketing imagination and practice could be brought to bear, it would soon earn the trust and respect of management by showing solid gains. The reader will have to decide for him- or herself how that can best be done, but one approach is to attack the new marketing missions of the online industry in highly creative and structured ways, while working behind the scenes to reshape the management environment.

INFORMED IMAGINATION

Creativity is universally recognized as one of the most desirable and undercultivated of all accomplishments. Yet it is profoundly distrusted, reviled, and criticized. Applying creativity to marketing issues is a business problem in its own right. In the online industry the creative level has to be improved and fostered if for no other reason than to meet the growing competitive challenges.

CONCLUSIONS

The industry is dominated by its pricing strategies, which determine both marketing strategy and how the company competes. Speculate for a moment on what cutting the apron strings might mean to growth. If marketing were free to price responsively to market and industry factors, new pricing schemes, marketing strategies, and buyer relationships might emerge that would be productive for all concerned.

The industry has gained a foothold and has begun to show signs of maturing. One of the real milestones will be when the industry switches its thinking from technology driven to market driven: this will result in much better treatment for the buyer and user. It could bring with it the keys to the kingdom if marketers rise, or are allowed to rise, to the opportunity. The inevitable changes that come with maturation will be more productive with professional marketing departments working to support and assure buyers and users that their interests are considered in all of the changes.

For the online services serving the up-scale markets that want and use complex knowledge products, many of their primary markets (e.g., national governments, large institutions, the professions, multinational finance, and business) are well penetrated by numbers of strong, highly competitive players. Penetration for the initial sale is nearly complete in the specialized and most profitable segments of the United States market. The full extent to which online services can be used (as opposed to the actual extent that they are used by these major customers) is unknown: but marketing managers fret that actual use is very low—in the 5–15 percent range of all possible use occasions. Marketing has not yet worked out a solid program for making this kind of cycling sale, regardless of the huge investment in user instruction and other techniques.

Because market penetration is uncomfortably complete in some of the best markets, many organizations are turning to new ventures and secondary markets in the hunt for new growth. Some of these markets are being slowly penetrated, but the start-up costs seem high when using marketing's current tool mix, which was developed for use in prime markets. With even the early returns from all precincts not yet in, many marketing questions go unanswered. In all markets, but especially in the tertiary markets, penetration may be stalled, pending the computer industry's ability to get its act together. Information utilities seem to be growing and thriving on a mix of home and business customers. They, too, of course, would benefit from revived computer sales, especially from a new generation of low-cost readily usable machines with built-in modems.

THE FUTURE

Growth from this point forward is not easy. Marketing will have to grow conceptually and operationally more powerful and trusted by devising and using new approaches to pricing, technology, markets, products, and services to win new markets, build use, and fend off the competition. It remains to be seen if marketing can be awarded a peerage in online management, but when the day comes that a top online marketer becomes CEO of one of the big online organizations, the competition and the rest of the industry will soon feel the heat.

INDEX

G

Gottsman, Edward, 34, 37

H

Harvard Business Review, 45

I

IBM, 1–2, 129
IMNET, 127
InfoLine, 8, 69–73, 126–27, 156–58, 197–205
information workers, 77
initial sales, 41–75
 and buyers, 43–44
 and marketing communications, 46–75
 and marketing issues, 44–46
 and omnibus brochures, 63–75
 and visual communications, 61–63

J

Jeffcoat, A. E., 209

K

knowledge workers, 77–84
KNOWLEDGE-INDEX, 191, 197
Kyodo News International, 127–28

L

Levitt, Theodore, 77–78
libraries and librarians, 22–23, 81–82
Lotus, 132–36

M

McCarthy Information Services, 126, 161–62
McCarthy Online, 115
McGraw-Hill, 153–56
McKenna, Regis, 139, 209
mailing lists, 181–83
mainframe, the, 3–5
management, 23–24

marketing communications, 46–75, 84–102, 117–72
 and benefits vs. technical merit and features in advertising, 117–28
 and corporate strategies, 168–72
 and current ideas and images to show benefits, 129–36
 and global advertising, 162–68
 and needs-gap analysis, 136–39
 and positioning, 139–41, 151–56, 161–62
 and pricing, 156–60
marketing tool mix, the, 117–215
 and direct marketing, 176–205
 and direct telemarketing, 205–9
 and public relations, 209–15
 and research and competitive analysis, 174–76
marketing in a working perspective, 15–21
 and the first sale, 34–37, 44–46
 and the information environment, 27–28
 and measures of success, 38–39
 and pricing, 29–34
 proactive, 17
 and second sale, 34–37, 77, 84–102, 105–9
 and user interest, 37–38
 zeroth law of, 16–17
Mead Data Central, 34
Mead's Lexis Service, 63–64, 142–46
menu-driven search, 6–8, 10
microcomputers, 12–13
mixed charges, 30–34
modem, 5, 12–13

N

needs-gap analysis, 136–39, 218
Neue Zurcher Zeitung, 210
NewsNet, 197

O

omnibus brochure (OB). *See* brochure

234764

T

telemarketing, 205–9
Telenet, 5
Telerate, 11, 163–68
Teletrade's City Business System,
    130–33
teletypewriters, 12
terminal software, 13–14
TextLine, 158–60
trade show, 62–63, 180
TYMNET, 5

U

Uninet, 5
user, online, 27–28, 78–79, 180

V

vanity charges, 20
variable charges, 29–33
vendors, defined, 3

W

Wall Street Journal, 210
Wang, 146–48, 151
Watson, Thomas, 1
Westlaw, 64–65, 143–46, 148